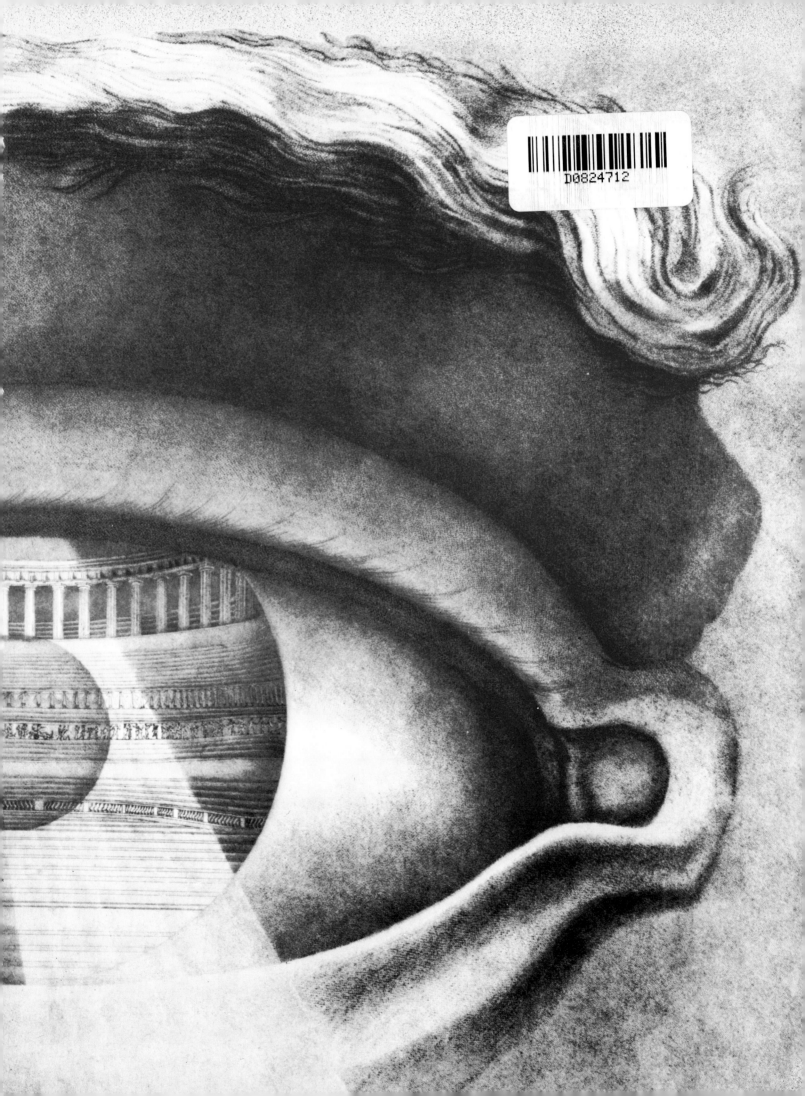

Quayle-Fushtey.

UTOPIA

UTOPIA

Ian Tod and Michael Wheeler

ORBIS PUBLISHING · London

Above: *Historical Monument of the American Republic* by Erastus Field
(Museum of Modern Art, Springfield, Mass., USA)

Frontispiece: *The Golden Age* by Lucas Cranach (1472–1553) (Bulloz)

Endpapers: Engraving by C. N. Ledoux (Paris 1804 ed.)
L'architecture considérée sous le rapport de l'art, des moeurs et de la legislation

© Orbis Publishing Ltd, London 1978
All rights reserved
Printed in Gt Britain by Hazell Watson & Viney
Hardback edition: ISBN 0 85613 049 4

Contents

Introduction

Utopia: an ideal commonwealth whose inhabitants exist under perfect conditions: book published by Sir T. More in 1516 describing imaginary island with perfect social and political system: ideally perfect place or state of things. Utopian; ardent but impractical reformer.

The reassuring language of a dictionary definition could never do justice to a word that has almost as many meanings as it has users, nor could it lead those users to agree. Utopia is a familiar everyday word, but it stands for many centuries of ideas, experiment and literature, and its history shows people at their most imaginative as well as at their most pedestrian. People have advocated it, hidden behind it, abused it, dreamed of it, or even tried to realize it. It is a blueprint, a novel, a prospectus, a political tract, a manifesto, a philosophical discourse, an actual state, or just a plain fantasy.

Is it possible to define it? Perhaps the only safe answer is that any attempt to do so would be hopeless . . . unrealistic, impracticable, impossible, doomed to failure, and a futile academic exercise—in fact, utopian. Yet to a great many people, the word has meant (and still means) quite the opposite, a source of hope, a guide to action, the embodiment of reason, the solution to social problems, the path to happiness, an ideal to be emulated, or the inevitable outcome of the process of history. In practice, one must accept the confusion and work within it.

Perhaps the question could be rephrased. What do utopias have in common? The answer is very little in detail, except, perhaps, for an almost universal dislike of lawyers, and there are even exceptions to that generalization. However, utopias *are* about how people should live, about human nature, and the meaning and purpose of life. And thus they deal with perennial problems; happiness, good and evil, authority, the state, religion, knowledge, work, sex, equality, liberty. Some utopias assume that people are inherently bad and that they need a state to prevent society breaking down in chaos. Others maintain that people are inherently good, and it is only institutions like a state that prevent them living in peace and co-operation. Some see the solution of social problems in the pursuit of material prosperity, whereas others see it in austerity and simplicity. Some advocate private property, but by far the majority advocate some form of communism, with equal access to the bounty of nature and equal status between people.

Utopias may be concerned with the happiness of the individuals in society, or with their ideal organization, and the two concerns don't always fit together very well. They are frequently associated with periods of great social upheaval, and so are concerned with the security of the body politic—the state—rather than individual happiness. Thus utopia, curiously, is rarely a very pleasant place to live.

But whatever the variety and confusion, utopias, in their reassessment of the organization of life, are concerned with three main relationships: firstly, people's relationships with each other—democracy and marriage for example—secondly, people's relationship with nature; and thirdly, people's relationship to their work. In selecting this short history from the vast array of utopian material, it is these three relationships that we have kept in mind.

If there is a dominant theme in this book it is that the dream of freedom in co-operation with nature, that takes its earliest form in the earthly paradise, has kept reappearing in opposition to the utopias that stress state power and stability. The conflict still rages, only today the stakes are greater, and the alternatives might well be 'utopia or oblivion'.

Left: The Tower of Babel by Pieter Breughel the Elder (1525/30–69). The story of its construction shows the folly of aspiring to Heaven in this life

The Earthly Paradise and the City of God

Ever since Adam and Eve were expelled from the Garden of Eden, people have dreamt of utopia. For most, it has been a comforting ideal in the distant past, the distant future or a distant corner of the earth. But for a great many others, it has been an epic voyage of discovery into the possible future—an inspiration and guide to the transformation of reality. People have attempted to realize it by experiment, example, reform, revolution, divine intervention or simply by withdrawing into the wilderness. Some have even hoped to construct it in steel and stone or gold and glass. Others have just laughed the whole idea of utopia to scorn.

Over the centuries the dreams have changed with the times. Frequently they have placed the security and health of the ideal society above the happiness of its members. Yet the dream of individual happiness keeps on emerging. It is with the earliest form of this dream—the search for an earthly paradise—that the story of utopia begins.

The Earthly Paradise

The earliest recorded journey in search of the earthly paradise was made by Gilgamesh, the legendary king of the city of Uruk, in ancient Sumeria. His story survives on stone tablets that date from around 2000 BC.

Gilgamesh was the last person likely to need the comforting dream of an ideal land in which all his problems would be solved. He was the most powerful, strong, wealthy and beautiful of men, holding unchallenged and absolute authority over the people of Uruk. The will and pleasure of Gilgamesh, however, did not always bring pleasure to his subjects, so

Left: Adam and Eve expelled from the garden of Eden—one of the earliest images of the ideal land of peace and plenty—as depicted by Giovanni di Paolo (c1410 to 82)

9

they begged the gods to send him a companion who would divert his excessive energies and appetites. This was Eukidu, the child of nature and wild man from the hills, who had been brought up amongst the animals, and all but matched Gilgamesh in beauty and strength. As arranged by the gods, they became inseparable comrades and together they performed many mighty deeds and surmounted many obstacles. In so doing, they offended one of the gods, who retaliated by striking Eukidu with a wasting sickness from which he eventually died. Gilgamesh was heart-broken and fell into despair. In desperation he set out to find Utnapishtim the Faraway, who was the only survivor of the deluge and had been granted eternal life by the gods.

The journey to Dilmun, where Utnapishtim lived, was long and difficult and (as subsequent utopians also discovered) did not turn out as he had hoped. He fought lions, scaled mountains and passed through days of total darkness. Everyone he met advised him to turn back or tried to divert him from his journey, but eventually he reached and crossed the river of Ocean, a touch of whose water meant instant death, and finally arrived in the earthly paradise where Utnapishtim lived in perpetual leisure and relaxation. In Dilmun, 'the croak of the raven was not heard, the bird of death did not utter the cry of death, the lion did not devour, the wolf did not rend the lamb, the dove did not mourn, there was no widow, no sickness, no old age, no lamentation'. In typical paradisical fashion, it was situated at the springing of the pure clear 'waters of the earth' with a perfect springtime climate and no strong winds or rain.

Gilgamesh had hoped to learn the secrets that would liberate him from his unhappy human predicament, but at every step in his journey was told that there was no escape and that he must accept mortality and the misfortunes of life. The message of Utnapishtim the Faraway was the same: 'There is no permanence. Do we build a house to stand for ever, do we seal a contract to hold for all time? . . . Does the flood-time of rivers endure? It is only the nymph of the dragonfly who sheds her larva and sees the sun in his glory. From the days of old there is no permanence.'

The epic of Gilgamesh expresses the futility of trying to escape the fetters of mortality and reflects a general pessimism in the cultures of the Euphrates Valley. The climate and floods made existence precarious and a shortage of material resources such as timber led to almost continuous war. But Dilmun itself contains nearly all the ingredients that has made the earthly paradise a source of hope throughout the world and also a subject for satire. *The True History* of the second century AD Roman author, Lucian, contains a parody of it that is hardly distinguishable from more serious accounts. His 'Island of the Blessed' has clear streams, flowery meadows, and beautiful woods. The grapes ripen every month and the trees yield crops of fruit 13 times a year. The city is built of gold and jewels and paved in ivory. No one grows any older, and the Elysian Fields themselves are meadows in the centre of a wood. There people are engaged in a continuous celebration of the pleasures of life—enjoying heterosexual and homosexual love-making, and drinking from twin springs of laughter and pleasure. They lie on beds of flowers with nightingales raining petals on them and the trees continually supplying wine.

Despite satire, the land of Dilmun, with its peace and tranquillity, freedom from labour, its eternal life and bountiful nature, reappears throughout history in popular legends of a promised land, either past or future. This earthly paradise is the perpetual response to perpetual hard times, the dream of people, from the Israelite slaves in Egypt to the American hobo, who want a break. It is the land 'where the sun shines on both sides of the hedge'. Although it appears in many different historical and cultural guises it is a feature of all societies, even when opposed by the dominant culture. It can be found in folk ballads such as the 'Song of Cockaygne':

> In Cokaygne we drink and eat
> Freely without care and sweat,
> The food is choice and clear the wine,
> At fourses and at supper time,
> I say again, and I dare swear,

Below: A colossal stone statue of Gilgamesh, dating from the eighth century BC, and found at Khorsabad, Iraq. Gilgamesh was the legendary king of Uruk who made an epic journey to Dilmun, the Sumerian land of eternal life

No land is like it anywhere,
Under heaven no land like this
Of such joy and endless bliss.

There is many a sweet sight,
All is day, there is no night,
There no quarrelling nor strife,
There no death, but endless life;
There no lack of food or cloth,
There no man or woman wroth. . . .
All is sporting, joy and glee,
Lucky the man that there may be.

Above: The Land of Cockaygne by Pieter Breughel the Elder. The painting depicts an ironic view of a utopia of unlimited leisure, food and drink: 'Under heaven no land like this of such joy and endless bliss'

The dream of the golden age has tended to come to the fore in periods of upheaval and popular rebellion. The Peasants' Revolt of 1381 was directed against serfdom and heavy taxation, but it was also sustained by the belief that England before the Norman Conquest had been a country of freedom and equality with every peasant cultivating his own plot in peace. They looked forward to a restoration of that situation. John Ball, one of the spokesmen, summed up this attitude when he asked, 'When Adam delved and Eve span, who was then the gentleman?' Matters would continue to get worse in England, he preached, until 'there be no villagers nor gentlemen, and there be no greater masters than we be'.

Another factor in the revolt, and one that frequently accompanies the belief in a golden age, was the expectation of the millennium. Both reappear regularly in the story of utopia. At the millennium, God would intervene directly in human affairs and cleanse the world of evil and injustice, people would become one with God, and the life that would follow resembles that in the earthly paradise. Indeed Heaven itself is frequently interwoven with the earthly paradise in the myths of the millennium.

The New Jerusalem

In Revelations 20, ii–viii, John the Divine describes how the devil would be bound for a thousand years, during which time the world would be ruled by the just who had suffered and died for Jesus Christ. At the end of the thousand years the devil would be released for a while and would go into the world and 'deceive the nations', creating misery and chaos. Finally God would intervene and throw the devil and his followers into a 'lake of fire and brimstone'. All the dead would rise up and be judged, the wicked would follow the devil into the lake and the rest live in 'a new heaven and a new earth' with a 'New Jerusalem, the Holy City'.

Inevitably, times of terrible suffering have been interpreted as the outbreak of the millennium, and the calculations that such a prophecy must engender have led many people to attempt to forecast it.

John's description of the new earth has all the ingredients of the paradise myth, with a pure river of life and a tree of 'life which bore twelve manner of fruits and yielded her fruit every month and the leaves of the tree were for the healing of the nations'. But it also relates back to the Kingdom of God as described by the Old Testament prophets. Ezekiel had described the New Jerusalem in detail, having the land divided equally among all people. According to Isaiah, the wilderness would become like 'Eden' and 'the desert like the garden of the lord; joy and gladness shall be found therein, thanksgiving and the voice of melody . . . the sun shall no more go down, neither shall the moon withdraw itself: for the lord shall be unto thee an everlasting light and thy god thy glory . . . the wolf and the lamb shall feed together, and the lion shall eat straw like the bullock'.

All these descriptions—and there are many more—enabled people to visualize heaven and the earthly paradise and they were augmented and embellished by the visions and discoveries of later saints and travellers. A sixth-century Irish missionary called Brendan, for example, after

Left: Hans Memlinc's fifteenth-century Flemish painting of the vision of Saint John the Divine as described in the Book of Revelations. His prophecies led many to expect a cataclysmic upheaval followed by eternal peace and plenty

Left: An ideal of an ordered life from a medieval manuscript. All were under the authority of the church and lived in harmony with nature and the seasons
Right: An idyllic country landscape painted by the sixteenth-century artist Simon Bering

returning from a sea voyage to the far north, reported seeing a land inhabited by the blessed with cathedrals of crystal and with no night. This relates closely to the description in Revelations: 'The city was pure gold, like unto glass . . . and had no need of the sun, neither of the moon to shine on it, for the glory of god did lighten it and the lamb is the light thereof . . . and the gates of it shall not be shut at all by day; for there shall be no night there'. Like the earthly paradise, the city of the New Jerusalem has been a symbol of hope and rebirth. This is common in times when upheavals have led to millennial interpretations—William Blake used it as a vehicle to prophesy the rebirth of his Albion, an England cleansed of inequality, corruption, aristocracy and other evils.

The City of God

The symbol of the heavenly city had another function in the medieval world apart from providing the comfort of an escape to paradise. In AD 410, when the city of Rome was captured and sacked by Alaric the Goth, the disintegration of the Roman Empire was complete and the illusion of Roman power could no longer be sustained. The end of the world was expected and many put the blame for the collapse on the relatively new Christian religion which, with its 'love' and 'brotherhood', had introduced principles that were incompatible with the maintenance of a strong state. The answer, they said, lay in a return to the old religions and to martial and heroic values.

Sparta and the Republic

When, during the Renaissance, Thomas More coined the word 'utopia', he did so, appropriately, from the Greek. Utopia means 'no-place'. However, 'eu-topia', pronounced the same way, means 'good place'. The word combines the ideal and the imaginative.

At this time, newly discovered Greek classical works were playing an important role in the social, cultural and intellectual changes of the Renaissance. The work of Plato was of particular importance, and the question of the state, ideal and actual, was one that occupied Plato throughout his life, beginning with the *Republic,* written around 394 BC.

Plato grew up during the Peloponnesian War which eroded the power of Athens and culminated in military defeat by Sparta in 404 BC. His speculations on the ideal state grew directly out of the success and power of Sparta. Indeed, it would be difficult to underestimate the influence of Sparta on utopian and political writers. It provided a respected classical precedent for ideas such as the state control of property, money, industry, education, morals and commerce, and also for ideas of sexual equality and the regulation of marriage and reproduction for the benefit of the community and state. Moreover it had few but simple laws, condemned luxury and regarded all change as a sign of weakness and imperfection. From Plato and More to Rousseau and Wells, it could be justifiably claimed that the story of utopia begins with the state of Sparta and the myths that grew out of its military supremacy.

The main literary source on Sparta is Plutarch's *Life of Lycurgus.* It was this work that was read by the writers of the Renaissance. Plutarch compiled it from previous works, so it is already a mixture of myth and

Left: A Roman mosaic depicting Plato with pupils from his Academy, discoursing on the ideal state

19

Below: Medallion of a Spartan warrior. The state of Sparta, organized as an army on a constant war footing, has been an ideal model for many theorists
Bottom: The vigour and health encouraged by a Spartan education is idealized in this nineteenth-century painting by Degas

history. Lycurgus reputedly founded, or re-established, the city state of Sparta, but its characteristics probably developed gradually over more than a century of introverted and isolationist policies. During the eighth century BC, Sparta, hungry for land and with limited access to the sea, had annexed the neighbouring state of Messenia. A century later, the Messenians tried to win their freedom by rebellion, but the movement was crushed. Thereafter a consciousness of internal instability permeated Spartan affairs. By organizing the state on a permanent war footing, they eventually achieved military supremacy over the whole of Greece.

The citizens as a whole were the fighting force, and although they exercised certain formalistic democratic rituals, they were, nonetheless, under military discipline. Citizenship depended firstly on birth, secondly on success in education and military training, and thirdly on the ability to conform.

Political power in Sparta was nominally held by two kings ruling with a senate of 28 elders, who were also supposed to provide a check to the power of the kings. They were elected by acclamation in an assembly of all the citizens which had power to reject or ratify laws, but not to instigate them, and which deliberated on matters of war and peace. In practice, however, power was held by a central committee of five men, the Ephorate, which presided over and controlled the business of both senate and assembly. By Greek reckoning, this was a 'mixed constitution', tending to tyranny but with a somewhat illusory democracy.

However, it was not the peculiarities of its political system that attracted people's attention to Sparta, but the social system and austerity that stemmed from the rigorous and single-minded pursuit of military efficiency. The system of Lycurgus was based on the redistribution of the land, not to provide equality for its own sake, but to promote unity among the ruling group and set the economic basis for a regime of austerity. Each citizen had enough land for his needs, but not enough to become wealthy. Thus the basis of citizenship was directly in the land. The system was rural and dispersed rather than urban; citizens received similar returns from their

land, and the absence of large holdings was designed to prevent those debilitating attacks of luxury to which the wealthy were so prone.

Further to this, a currency reform banned gold and silver and replaced them with iron bars. Foreign exchange virtually ceased, foreigners themselves were deported, and travel and novelty were suppressed. In short, anything that might disturb the plan was erased. The citizens were almost wholly engaged in military exercise, learning and teaching; and productive labour was forbidden. Not even much craftsmanship was allowed: laws directed that ceilings be made only with the axe and doors with the saw.

As a further discouragement to domesticity, Lycurgus instituted common messes of about 15 persons. Attendance was compulsory and to be banned from the mess was tantamount to losing citizenship. The men slept in dormitories, both before and after marriage. Indeed, the institution of marriage was virtually dissolved so that private affections might not develop and weaken the love of the state. Women escaped the family only to become breeding machines, and such marriage regulations as existed seem to have been designed to promote fertility. Marriage was allowed for women at 20 and for men at 26. Meetings between partners were primarily for sex and some couples even had children before they got around to meeting during the daytime. Similarly, adultery was not considered a crime nor even discouraged—children were seen as the property of the state, which saw no sense in curtailing any enthusiastic intercourse that might breed healthy little Spartans. At birth each child was inspected by the oldest men. If it was strong and healthy it was allocated a plot of land and its education arranged for. If not, it was thrown into a deep cavern on the principle that 'its life could be no advantage to itself or to the public, since nature had not given it first any strength or goodness of constitution'.

At the age of seven the male children were formed into companies for their education, and leaders, to whom complete obedience was expected, were selected from amongst them. Non-military learning and culture was kept to a minimum and 'all the rest of their education was calculated to make them subject to command, to endure labour, to fight and to conquer'. They were allowed one garment, made their own shelter and generally lived in deprivation. At the age of 12, their regime tightened up, punishment and deprivation were intensified and war games were introduced, sometimes involving the mass murder of slaves. Female education followed similar lines though with more of an athletic than a military bent, so that 'thus fortified by exercise, they might better support the pangs of childbirth and be delivered with safety'.

Should the grown Spartan soldier-citizen have any nagging problems of self-esteem, the continued presence of the Helots (slaves) provided ample evidence of Spartan superiority, reinforced at times by forcing the Helots into drunkenness and humiliating antics.

In the idealized Sparta that has influenced many utopians, the system is praised for its basic, simple and austere life (Spartan simplicity); its communism; its destruction of the family; its rural rather than urban basis; its 'democracy'; and its dedication to the collective rather than the individual. It was not a state that valued the production of culture, but as a military machine it was for a time unbeatable, resoundingly defeating the Athenian democracy that had produced, under the influence of Pericles, the golden age of Greek art. Pericles had claimed that Athens should be the model for the rest of Greece. After his death in 429 BC, the Athenian democracy that he dominated became progressively weaker until Athenians themselves were looking elsewhere—mainly to Sparta—in order to remodel their own state.

Plato's Republic

The typical Greek state was situated at the mouth of a narrow valley with direct access to the sea. Communication was easier by sea than by land, and the cities, restricted as they were by the natural topography, relieved the pressures of population through a policy of colonization—they founded new cities on virgin sites. Thus the Greeks were highly conscious of, and practised in, constitution-making, and consultants were often

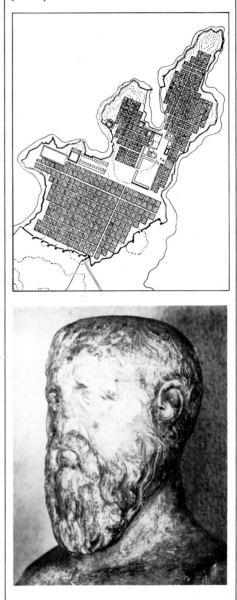

Below: Miletus, home of the planner Hippodamus—the ideal regular plan to complement the ideal regulated constitution Bottom: Plato (428/27–348/47 BC). Just as a sick person required the specialist attention of a doctor, he argued, so also the body politic needed the wise rule of philosophers

Overleaf: The Acropolis was the product of Periclean Athens, the Golden Age of Greek Democracy. Although Athens has provided an ideal for democracy, it is strange that many utopians have turned for inspiration to its totalitarian neighbour, Sparta

brought in when a new colony was being planned. The organization of space and the organization of politics went hand in hand and as much time was spent on social philosophy as on town planning.

Plato's *Republic* did not appear alone then, but is merely the most influential and well-known work in what was almost a national pastime. Nor is it his final word, for he modified it and suggested alterations in his later works, although he is constant in his opposition to the sophists, who advocate greater freedom as the solution to the problems of Athenian life, and supported the traditional belief in a golden age where people lived in complete freedom and equality.

This sanguine vision is expressed in the slightly later utopia of Zeno—a community of all mankind, without states, political institutions or class distinctions. Marriage, temples, law-courts and money are all abolished and education is reformed. There are no over-grand state buildings, just the virtue of its inhabitants, living a communal life presided over by Eros, god of friendship and concord. Zeno believed that all could reach a state of virtue and wisdom and that the senses of justice and responsibility were the essential natural instincts. Plato, looking over his shoulder towards Sparta, had a fundamentally different view of human nature and believed, moreover, that it could do with a helping hand. As a philosopher, he did not consider that the *Republic* could be realized on earth, but that it embodied the principles that state-makers should follow, the ideal towards which they should strive.

He argued, by analogy, that, just as a sick person needed a doctor, and it was natural for some to be healers and some to be healed, so it was natural for some to be rulers and some to be ruled. Zeno, in contrast, argued, also from nature, that everyone should be their own ruler. However, Platonic distinctions did not mean that people inevitably fell into the correct category. Not any old fool could rule, nor any group, and a mass of incompetent, ignorant fools would make an incompetent ignorant ruler. Plato had little sympathy for the Athenian democracy that had condemned and executed his teacher Socrates. Ruling was an art, just as medicine was an art; and as doctors must be trained, so must rulers.

Plato divided the people of the Republic (excluding slaves) into three orders: at the top were the Rulers, with legislative and deliberative power; under them, but closely allied, came the Auxiliaries, with executive and military responsibility—these two groups together form the Guardians; thirdly, without any proper title, came the farmers, artisans and traders who have productive duties. This division is based on 'natural capacities' and is the necessary basis for a happy society, since happiness lies in the virtuous exercise of natural gifts. However, just in case the people will not see the natural justice of this division, Plato felt it necessary to construct a myth to placate them and keep them in their place. (Presumably the truths of philosophy are beyond such people, so the myths of philosophers must do.) People are born, the myth goes, with metal in their hearts—gold, silver or iron in varying proportions. Those with gold in their hearts are destined to be Rulers, those with silver to be Auxiliaries and those with iron to toil, but not so hard as the slaves, who presumably have no metal in them whatsoever.

Apart from putting them in their place, Plato has no special prescription for the people of iron, and the bulk of the *Republic* is concerned with the education and way of life of the Guardians. The education of a Guardian begins at an early age with the reading of approved stories. As children cannot distinguish the allegorical from the literal, stories and myths must be specially invented. In these stories the gods would do no evil, for the child must associate heaven only with what is good. To make them brave and unafraid of death, stories about the underworld are to be cleaned up so that it appears a good rather than a gloomy place; similarly reference to 'bewailing the dead' should be removed. Future Guardians must be serious, so the tales should not be too humorous, and Homer's occasional references to the 'unquenchable laughter' of the gods must go.

Honesty must be valued highly, and so must deception, which is useful to mankind as a medicine. As such it should be handled and prescribed only by the physicians, i.e. the Guardians. It follows that, while for a person

Above: Socrates Teaching by H. Bates. This portrays the situation in Plato's Republic, which proceeds as a dialogue between Socrates and his friends. Aristophanes in The Birds satirized utopian speculation: 'Before you founded your city,' he wrote, 'everyone was Sparta-mad, long hair, empty bellies, grubby, Socratizing, staff in hand'

to lie to the Guardians is equivalent to mutiny on a ship, the Guardian has the privilege and responsibility of using falsehood for the benefit of the commonwealth. To carry such a burden the Guardian will need self-control, and consequently the literature must be modified to emphasize examples of fortitude and remove any examples of heroes succumbing to temptation, human frailty or base impulses.

In all things, such as music, literature and the arts, Plato demanded excellence and purity of form and content. Poets must be forced to express noble character, architects, painters, weavers and all other craftworkers must leave out 'baseness, licence, meanness or unseemliness', or they will be forbidden to practise, and Guardians must not grow up 'among representations of moral deformity'.In education, Plato is a materialist as to technique, but even so, firmly believes in mind over matter. Bodily exercise is not so much useful for muscular strength as for stimulating the soul, since exercise alone results in 'savage ignorance' and too much mindwork and relaxation 'will result in over softness: the right training will produce a gentleness that is steady and disciplined'.

Moderation and temperance is also encouraged in all things, especially in relation to sexual pleasure where the young Guardian runs a high risk of frenzy. A law prescribes that 'a lover may seek the company of his beloved and, with his consent, kiss and embrace him like a son, with honourable intent, but must never be suspected of any further familiarity, on pain of being thought ill-bred and without any delicacy of feeling'. It is not clear whether Plato is trying to legislate passion purely out of homosexual relationships, but sexual intercourse was certainly not considered in terms of love and was to be strictly rationed and controlled in the interests, as always, of the state.

The Guardians were to be a single interrelated group—to call it a 'family' would be to stretch both the productive and biological usage of the word too far. The private home no longer exists so that there is no tendency for Guardians to prefer private interests against public—in fact there is virtually no private interest at all. No man or woman may set up home together and no parent may know their own child, or vice versa.

Breeding is regulated entirely by the rulers who mate only the best specimens and try to achieve a stable population. Only people in their prime are selected (20 to 40 for women and 25 to 55 for men) and special festivals were to be instituted where mating would be preceded by appropriate sacrifices, poetry and music. Plato recognizes that this system might be the cause of some dissatisfaction among those who were not selected, so the exercise is to be dressed up as a lottery so that inferior breeding stock could blame their frustrations on the vagaries of fortune. It was an 'offence against divine and human law' to produce children outside the prescribed framework, but people outside the set ages and infertile women were allowed sex with whomever they wished.

Newborn children were to be removed immediately from their mothers and taken to a common nursery. Care should be taken that the mothers would be unable to identify their own children when they arrived for breast-feeding. As to parentage, all parents from a particular festival were mothers and fathers to all the children, and all that group of children were considered brothers and sisters. Any children who were not up to scratch would be quietly removed, presumably to the ranks of Irons, where they at least had the opportunity to manage their own personal affairs.

Just as he allowed no private relationship or exclusive possession between men and women, Plato allowed no private property in goods, feeling that the effects of private wealth were always corrupting, not so so much to the individuals concerned as to the unity of the state. People should not be allowed to develop any private interest lest that would in time work against the public interest.

In the case of Sparta, this unity was achieved by the equal distribution of all the land, whereas in the *Republic* the Guardians own all property in common. Women in the *Republic* are equal to the men, and have equal opportunity to rule, and therefore to participate in ownership. (Indeed, it is in his prescription for equality of the sexes that Plato is most radical. Men and women receive the same education, both can go to war and both can be selected for training as Rulers—although in Athens at the time of Plato women held a very secondary and secluded position.) But in both cases it is a simple, austere and disciplined life. Happiness lay in fulfilling one's duties and being respected and honoured for it.

Plato's prescription of a ruling class practising communism, rigorous and controlled education, abolition of the family and eugenics reappears in various guises throughout the story of utopia. So does his notion of the philosopher king who tops the heap of disinterested, ideal and virtuous guardians.

> Unless either philosophers become kings . . . or those who are now indeed kings come to be inspired with a desire for wisdom; unless, that is to say, political power and philosophy meet together . . . there can be no rest from troubles . . for all mankind.

After various political consulting and educational positions, mainly at Syracuse in Sicily, Plato returned to Athens and set up his Academy. He never found a philosopher king, but his pupil, Aristotle, became tutor to Alexander the Great. The main classical example of a ruling caste similar to the Guardians comes not from Greece but Sicily, and predates Plato. The Pythagorean Brotherhood came to control several cities, such as Cortona and Metapontum, but eventually the people rebelled and they were massacred. Iron proved to be stronger than silver or gold.

Top: Pythagoras—the Pythagorean Brotherhood formed a ruling élite similar to Plato's Guardians
Above: Pericles (b. 494 BC), general, orator, statesman and charismatic leader of democratic Athens. His death in 429 marked the end of the golden age

The Renaissance City State

The 200 years following AD 1400 saw medieval Europe transformed by the Renaissance and Reformation. In particular, the cohesive institution of the Middle Ages, the church, with its vast international bureaucracy of clerics, was finally and irrevocably split in the Reformation. Its dominance of intellectual, social, economic and political life was broken, releasing the potential of a host of new and revived ideas, relationships and institutions, and producing a flood of innovation and invention. In the process of this upheaval, interest shifted from the heavenly to the earthly paradise and the ideal secular state again became an object of debate and speculation. The classical tradition of the Greek state was revived in the idealizations of the Italian city state, in the comprehensive *Utopia* of Thomas More, and in Campanella's *City of the Sun*. Campanella proposed a new political and religious synthesis, a new European commonwealth, to replace Christendom and the Holy Roman Empire. The revival of classical learning was just one aspect of the Renaissance, but it was a vitally important aspect with direct and obvious results in the culture of the time. The classics were evidence of a different civilization, and people came to see in them possible alternatives and solutions to the problems of a medieval world whose equilibrium had been irreversibly dissolved. If classicism took root it was because the ground had been prepared through the movements, catastrophes and events of the medieval world itself. The Crusades of the twelfth and thirteenth centuries had brought people into contact with foreign nations, customs, religions and cultures. In the fifteenth century improvements in the design of ships made voyages of discovery and the expansion of trade possible.

Left: The School of Athens (c1509) by Raphael. Plato's Academy has become peopled by the new learned élite of the Renaissance, the Humanists

27

The voyages of Cabot, Vasco de Gama, Columbus, Vespucci and others brought gold and silver, but they also transformed people's image of the world with knowledge and fantastic stories of lands and peoples whose existence had never even been suspected. For example, although the works of classical geographers such as Ptolemy were in the libraries, the medieval world map was symbolic, centred on Jerusalem for theological reasons. A description of the actual physical relationship between places or the real shape of the world was low down on the list of priorities for the medieval map-maker, just as geometrical perspective was not a primary concern of the artist. Similarly, the medieval view of the solar system was based on theology as well as observation, hence the consternation when Galileo showed that the Milky Way, previously believed to contain the heavenly mansions of the blessed, was in fact a collection of discrete stars.

During the fourteenth century, Europe had been ravaged by bubonic plague, supposedly brought from the East by ship-borne rats. It reduced Europe's population drastically, another factor undermining the system of tied labour which had underpinned feudal society. Slowly the position of the towns with their 'free' citizens was strengthened against the feudal aristocracy, beginning the long transformation from feudal work relationships to modern wage labour. In Italy the towns became the City State and it was the ruling families, such as the Medici in Florence, who fostered the revival of classical learning.

The fourteenth and fifteenth centuries saw a continuous immigration of scholars from the East, refugees from the Ottoman Turks whose empire expansion culminated in the fall of Constantinople in 1456. These scholars, mainly Greek, brought with them valuable manuscripts of the ancient classics. They were welcomed in the city states, joined the universities and set up schools which reached a new secular audience.

As teachers of Greek and Latin, they were described as 'Humanistica', hence their students, the pioneers of the Renaissance, have been described

Below: Amerigo Vespucci (1451–1512), the Florentine navigator after whom America is named. Like many of his fellow navigators he expected to find the Earthly Paradise

as 'humanists', students of the ancient classics. But the term has come also to encompass their concern for the individual, for creativity, for free enquiry and for the sensual material world as opposed to the limited spiritual world of the Middle Ages with its dependence on religious authority and divine revelation. The humanists were a new intellectual élite, for they were a secular group who depended on the patronage of the wealthy merchants and so were intellectually and materially independent of the church.

The introduction of printing and paper was also enormously important and struck a great blow at the authority of the church. Criticism of the church was growing, for its corruption, its excessive wealth and land ownership, its monopoly of doctrine, and the restriction of the Bible to Latin, and so to the educated few. Printing enabled these criticisms to become widespread and to cross national borders, thus making possible the transition from local disturbance to international upheaval.

It was in this atmosphere of excitement and change, but also of anxiety and disorder, that the tradition of speculation in ideal states was revived. In particular, the Englishman, Thomas More, wrote the book that has given its name to the whole tradition, *Utopia*.

Utopia

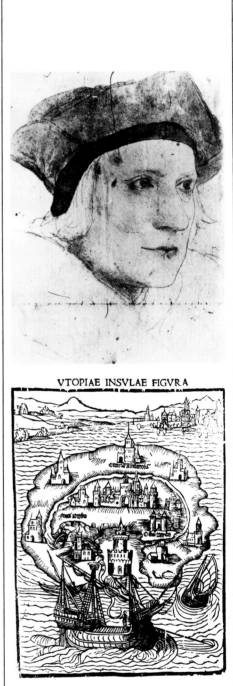

VTOPIAE INSVLAE FIGVRA

When Thomas More wrote *Utopia* during 1515 and 1516, he was writing, as it were, in the lull before the storm. The first phase of the Renaissance was over and the Reformation was about to break. The pioneer architects, Brunelleschi, Alberti and Bramante, were dead, Michelangelo had just completed the Sistine Chapel and was working on the completion of St Peter's, Leonardo da Vinci had only three years to live and Raphael, four. Machiavelli had completed *The Prince* in 1513 and the Medicis had just returned to Florence after 20 years' exile following the short puritanical reign of Savonarola. More was directly linked to the Italian humanist tradition through his teacher at Oxford University, Grocyn, who had studied at Florence and Rome. But he was also a close friend of Erasmus, whose outspoken criticism of the church has been described as the egg that Luther hatched when he launched the Reformation. In 1517, one year after the completion of *Utopia*, Luther published his 95 theses, and the subsequent movement put an end to the hopes of men such as More and Erasmus that reform in the church might be achieved without a final split.

From the moment of its publication in Louvain, *Utopia* has been the subject of acclaim and argument. Within two years, three more editions had appeared, all of them in the original Latin, the international language of scholars, as well as the church. Clearly it was not a book for popular consumption and More made no attempt to translate it into English or to publish it in England. An English language edition eventually appeared in 1551, 16 years after his execution by Henry VIII.

In *Utopia* More does everything to confer authenticity on his story, by paying great attention to detail and even supplying a Utopian alphabet and an example of Utopian poetry. However, in the derivation of names of the places and people, he exposes the hoax to those scholars, far fewer than the Latin readers, who were conversant with Greek. Utopia, as we have pointed out, is a Greek pun; the river Anider means 'no water', the city Amanote means 'dream town' and the storyteller himself is called Raphael Hythlodae, 'dispenser of nonsense'.

More begins by describing how, on a diplomatic visit to Holland, his friend, Peter Gilles, had introduced him to Hythlodae, a wealthy and educated man, conversant with Plato. Hythlodae had decided to see the world and had made several voyages with the explorer, Amerigo Vespucci, who had published two well-known accounts of his journeys, *New World* (1505) and *Four Voyages* (1507). Like most of the explorers, he returned with fabulous tales of monsters and savages, and also of paradise. Such stories were to be expected in tales told by mariners and as Hythlodae claimed to be one of 24 sailers left behind by Vespucci in 1504, an incident recorded in *Four Voyages,* the credibility of his tale is doubly confirmed.

Top: This sympathetic sketch of Thomas More (1478–1535) by Holbein, was made at the height of More's political career
Above: Woodcut of the island of Utopia as it appeared on the frontispiece of the first edition published in Louvain 1516

Above: Utopia, from the Basle edition of 1518. Again it shows a medieval landscape very different from the regular planning described by More and being proclaimed and practised in Italy at the time

However, More's *Utopia* is not a paradise myth, but a vehicle for comments on his own society, and to tell the story via a dispenser of nonsense was not only a joke, but also a way of protecting himself from any dangerous consequences of being too outspoken. More was so successful in this that people are still divided as to whether he personally favoured the institutions he described, or whether it is wholly satirical, or a bit of both.

During the first part of their conversation, More, Gilles and Hythlodae discuss the state of the world and in particular the state of England. Raphael Hythlodae condemns the widespread use of the death penalty for theft as too severe, unjust and, in any case, ineffectual as a deterrent. He argues that people do not steal from a free choice but from necessity, which he explains with reference to both ends of feudal society. In the first place most noblemen were parasites, while, for the mass of the rural population, land enclosure and the introduction of sheep farming was ruining their means of subsistence, forcing them to steal in order to survive. The solution to the first group of thieves was to cut out the parasites, but the solution to the second was a new agricultural economy.

> Make a law that anyone responsible for demolishing a farm or a county town must either rebuild it himself or else hand over the land to someone who is willing to do so. Stop the rich from cornering markets and establishing virtual monopoly. Reduce the number of people who are kept doing nothing. Divide agriculture and the wool industry so that there's plenty of honest useful work for the great army of unemployed.

The second part is devoted to a full description of Utopia, a country whose 'way of life provides not only the happiest basis for a civilized community, but also one which, in all human probability, will last forever'.

Utopia is an island, off the coast of Somewhere. About 100,000 square miles in area, it is shaped like a huge crescent the tips of which almost meet so that the island itself encloses a huge natural lagoon and harbour. Originally it had been connected to the mainland but Utopas, the conqueror of the land and the founder of its civilization, had organized a gigantic dig to separate it and so make his conquest secure.

The country is divided into 54 towns, all as identical as the topography allows, and each surrounded by about 1,600 square miles of land to provide food for their 80,000 or so inhabitants (this total being roughly England's population at the time). Raphael describes the capital Amanote, chosen for its central position and easy accessibility by land and sea, but his description does equally well for the other towns for, as he says, 'when you've seen one of them, you've seen them all'. Amanote is heavily fortified and regularly planned, with four quarters, each with a market, and its hospital outside the walls. The streets are wide and straight, between three-storey, flat-roofed houses with glass or linen windows and interspersed with a larger communal building for every 30 houses.

Each house has an extensive garden at the rear and Utopians are 'keen gardeners, not only because they enjoy it but because there are interstreet competitions for the best kept garden. It would be hard to find any feature of the town more calculated to give pleasure and profit to the community'. Housing illustrates well the Utopian attitude to material goods. There is no shortage and very little new construction, for the houses are well built and continually maintained, and though they are comfortable they are also basic and lacking in luxury. No houses are privately owned, they are always open and people can go in and out of any house at will. 'The houses themselves are allocated by lot and changed around every ten years.'

Clothing, too, is basic and long-lasting, but sufficient—everyone has a leather work outfit, a natural-coloured woollen cloak, white linen underwear and a linen shirt. Utopians do not value conventional riches in the slightest and their use of precious stones and metals for chains and chamber pots is designed to instil an aversion rather than a lust for possession.

More departs from precedent and from many other communist utopias in making the family the basis of a communist society. He attempts to strike a balance between a strong and sacrosanct family and the cohesion of the community, and to do so draws on the examples of the medieval urban family and the religious community. The monogamous family, paternal, patriarchial, extended, procreative and productive is the basic unit in the pyramid of Utopian society. He regards each family or household as an economic and biological unit. In the town it has a minimum of ten adults, a maximum of 16 and its members are all engaged in one of the trades. Domestic trades, such as spinning, are done by the women of each household. If the numbers exceed 16, or if a person wants to follow a different trade, then they are allocated to other households. Wives join their husbands' household for 'women's work is the same everywhere'. All the goods produced are sent to a communal warehouse and all materials can be collected from there with no payment.

In the country, the household is much larger with at least 40 adults and two slaves, for everyone is obliged to take a turn at agricultural work before they take up their allotted trade, and at harvest time, extra workers are drafted in from the towns. Both rural and urban families are strictly paternal: 'Each household comes under the authority of the oldest male. Wives are subordinate to their husbands, children to their parents and younger people generally to their elders.' At the end of each month, in preparation for the religious festivals, 'Wives kneel down at home before their husbands, and children before their parents, to confess all their sins of omission and commission and ask to be forgiven. This gets rid of any little grudges that may have clouded the domestic atmosphere, so that everyone can attend divine service with an absolutely clear mind.'

Marriage is allowed at 18 for women and 22 for men and must be approved by the parents. But, before any agreement is made, 'the prospective bride, no matter whether she's a spinster or a widow, is exhibited stark naked to the prospective bridegroom by a respectable married woman, and a suitable male chaperone shows the bridegroom naked to the bride'. The reasoning behind this custom makes it clear that this is mainly for the benefit of the males who have most to gain in the marriage arrangement: 'When you're buying a horse, and there's nothing at stake but a small sum of money, you take every possible precaution . . . but when you're choosing a wife, an article that for better or worse has got to last you a lifetime, you're unbelievably careless. You don't even bother to take off its wrappings.' Marriage, once made, is final, and, 'if she turns ugly after the wedding, he must just resign himself to his fate—but one does need some legal protection against marriage under false pretences'.

Divorce is only allowed in extreme circumstances; it may, for instance, be permitted to the innocent partner in adultery cases. The adulterers, however, are sentenced to slavery 'of the most unpleasant type', and although sufficient remorse might win pardon from a first offence, 'a second conviction means capital punishment'. Clearly the Utopian laws discourage sexual relationships outside the institution of marriage. Indeed, anyone involved in premarital sex must forfeit the right to marriage at all, and attempts at seduction are punished as severely as if they had succeeded:

> The Utopians are particularly strict about that kind of thing, because they think very few people would want to get married— which means spending one's whole life with the same person, and putting up with all the inconveniences that this involved— if they weren't carefully prevented from having any sexual intercourse otherwise.

The social unit is of equal importance, and just as the family is maintained by the necessity of production, the social unit is maintained by the necessity of eating. People eat in groups of 30 households who share communal facilities in the enlarged household of an elected magistrate called the Syphogrant. Thus, twice a day, at lunch and supper, up to 500 adults eat together in a social group that cuts right across the family structure. Men and women sit at separate tables, with the Syphogrant and his wife at a high table on a raised dais. Seats are allocated so that young and old are

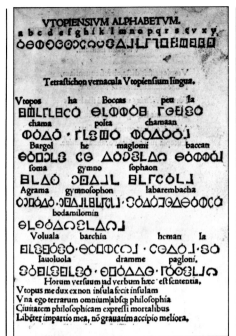

Above: One reader of Utopia *wondered why people thought More clever, when he only wrote down what he had been told. More's elaborate hoax, transparent to Greek readers but not obvious to the more numerous Latin readers, included a Utopian alphabet and an example of Utopian verse*

intermixed, so that 'respect for the older generation tends to discourage bad behaviour among the younger ones'. Meanwhile, the youngest children eat in a separate nursery and all the waiting at table is done by the older children up to the time they are married. They serve the eldest members first and with the best food, so reinforcing the principle of respect for age: 'If there's not enough of some particular delicacy to go round, the older ones share their helpings, as they think fit, with their neighbours.'

The position of the Syphogrants in relation to their 30 families is similar to that of the father within each individual family. Their chief business—in fact practically their only business—is to see that everyone gets on with his job. They are also the key elected magistrates in the political system. Every ten magistrates will elect a senior magistrate, called a Tranibor, whose job it is to act as cabinet to the town mayor, also elected by the Syphogrants, but for life.

Care is taken throughout the system to minimize the possibilities for corruption. If any person tries to canvass any office, then they are automatically disqualified from public service for life. Magistrates have no special privileges or uniform to mark them out from other people, but the mayor is always preceded in public by a person carrying a sheaf of corn. All decisions in cabinet must be discussed for at least three days, and, even so, major decisions are referred to a general council of the Syphogrants. As an additional check, a law forbids any loose discussion of government matters outside the council itself—and the penalty is death.

Although mayor and Tranibors are elected, they are all drawn from an intelligentsia that has been selected in the schools, and they are the only people in the community excused from manual work, but even this privilege can be withdrawn by the Syphogrants. For though intellectual pursuits are valued very highly, they would not give the intellectuals absolute power. In fact, they would give no one absolute power, and in the political system proposed for Utopia, More develops and cleans up the democracy of the independent medieval town, in marked contrast to the absolute monarchs and despots who were consolidating power throughout Europe in the early sixteenth century.

Despite the democratic structure, Utopians lead a strictly regulated life, constantly under the surveillance of the magistrates they have elected, or who were elected at least by the fathers of the households.

> There's never any excuse for idleness. There are also no wine-taverns, no ale houses, no brothels, no opportunities for seduction, no secret meeting-places. Everyone has his eye on you, so you're practically forced to get on with your job and make some proper use of your spare time.

Travel, too, is strictly controlled and anyone wanting to go to another town must obtain a pass from the mayor. They must make the journey in a group, not alone, and once they arrive they must take up their trade again within 24 hours. The punishments for wandering around in the country without a pass are severe, with slavery for a second offence.

Utopian law, though short and simple, is also rigid and implacable, and makes as widespread a use of slavery as contemporary society made of the death penalty. Clearly, the inhabitants of More's ideal state have little faith in the natural perfectibility of human nature. Slavery is institutionalized, not only by the law, but because work has been so arranged that slavery is necessary. Slaves do all the work that citizens find menial or degrading, like hunting, butchery, roadmending and cleaning, and it is this slave labour that frees the citizens for their productive and fulfilling trades. The slaves themselves are Utopian convicts, or, much more often, condemned criminals from other countries, who are acquired in large numbers sometimes for a small payment but usually for nothing. Both types of slaves are kept hard at work in chain-gangs, 'although Utopians are treated worse than foreigners'. Thus the Utopian democracy, just like the Spartan and Athenian 'democracy' is supported by slave labour, and the failure of some of its citizens is necessary to maintain a civilized and leisured life for the rest.

Although they only work a six-hour day, Utopians are not encouraged to idle away their leisure time. They are expected 'not to waste their time in idleness or self-indulgence, but to make good use of it in some congenial activity'. Dice and cards, and any other game that might be a temptation to gambling are prohibited, but they have two games similar to chess, and they favour music, further education, elevating conversation and religion. Those without an intellectual bent spend much of their leisure time 'back in the workshops' for the Utopians, like More himself, are 'particularly fond of the mental pleasures', which they consider to be of a higher order than merely physical pleasures such as 'itching, eating, drinking, rubbing and scratching'. They believe that reason is the essential part of any 'higher pleasure' and that true happiness comes only from mental pleasures rather than the pleasures of physical gratification.

Religion is based on reason just as is their idea of happiness, for Utopians, as Hythlodae explains, do not have the convenience of Divine Revelation, and have to rely on observation and deduction. As a result they have many religions, but without constriction or competition, for they practise religious tolerance to the extent that anyone who becomes too heated about religious matters is automatically banished.

> There are sun worshippers, moon worshippers and worshippers
> of various other planets. . . . However, the vast majority take
> the much more sensible view that there is a single divine power,
> unknown, eternal, infinite, inexplicable and quite beyond the
> grasp of the human mind, diffused throughout the universe of
> ours, not as a physical substance but as an active force. This
> power they call 'The Parent'.

The religious system proposed by More was possibly *Utopia's* most radical aspect for his immediate contemporaries. In the face of a wealthy, dogmatic, hierarchical church, More proposes a natural religion, with male and female priests elected by the congregation and complete religious tolerance, practised by a communist community. It is like an early Christian community, but without Christ or the church. Many Utopians became converted to Christianity by Hythlodae and his friends and were baptized, but, as there was no priest in their party they could have no access to the other Catholic sacraments. Again, there is the suggestion, on the eve of the Reformation, that the officers and rituals of the church were unnecessary to the life of a good Christian.

Despite the proposals of *Utopia,* when More himself became Chancellor of England, 13 years later, he was no more tolerant in religious matters than his predecessors. Executions for heresy continued under his rule, and he was a vituperative critic of Luther, behaviour which would have led to his expulsion from Utopia.

Like the classical Greek states, the Utopians solve the problems of population growth by setting up colonies 'at the nearest point on the mainland where there is a large area that hasn't been cultivated by the local inhabitants'. They allow the indigenous population to join in their colony if they wish, otherwise they are expelled—for the Utopians believe that it is unjust for the natives to hold on to land that they are not using to the full. This principle of 'natural justice' permeates all Utopian foreign policy, and they have taken on the role of international policemen in their part of the world. Many nations even choose to have Utopians run their country—a wise move, 'for the welfare of a state depends entirely on the quality of its administrators, and the Utopians are obviously ideal for the job', since, having no material ambitions, they are incorruptible.

Such colonies are called 'allies', but they also recognize 'friendly powers' whom they help out with other forms of aid—if necessary with military support, though they prefer not to go to war, except in self-defence. In practice, their conflicts rarely get to the point of Utopians losing blood. In the first place, they use psychological warfare to demoralize the opposition, and offer large sums of money to anyone who will turn in the enemies' leaders. If that fails, then troops, not from Utopia but mercenaries from Venalia, are sent in to do battle.

If the supply of Venalians runs out, then the Utopians turn to the friendly powers for fighters, and finally to their own citizens, both men and women, who form a volunteer army. Needless to say, they always win, are magnanimous in victory, kill only the offending leaders, always send the bill to the defeated rather than the country they helped, and even help out the defeated power with Utopian administrators.

It is hardly surprising that the inhabitants of the ideal state should consider that their ways and culture are infinitely superior to those of other nations. This nationalism, not to say chauvinism, is one of the few aspects of More's creation that is characteristic of the Renaissance. More may quote Plato and other classical authors, but the key institutions of Utopia are derived from medieval society, and it is ruled by a democratically elected magistracy rather than a self-selected ruling caste. If Utopia is intended to indicate solutions to the social upheavals of the day, it is surprising how lightly it carries More's classical learning, for the prescriptions preserve and develop the institutions of the medieval world rather than substitute models based on classical precedent.

Below: Lorenzetti's The City of Good Government, *a medieval image of democratic government through guilds and magistrates, the system described by More*
Right: Niccolo Machiavelli (1469–1527) whose famous book, The Prince, *was a guide to power and its use for the new Renaissance rulers*

The Ideal City

It is possible that More was stimulated to write *Utopia* partly by the appearance of Machiavelli's *The Prince* in 1513. The two works could hardly be more different. While *Utopia* is an exploration of how medieval institutions can be developed to create a stable and successful society for almost all its members, *The Prince* is a lesson on expediency—how an individual can take power and hold on to it. Concerned with power politics, it is a handbook of techniques, derived from the ancients but also from the history of the city state in the previous hundred years. The influence of Plato is seen far more positively in Machiavelli and the Italian humanists than in More. Both Plato and Machiavelli are concerned with the ruling class and both would use whatever violence or cynical deception was necessary to preserve their power at home.

The Utopians, by comparison, are angelic. *Utopia* stresses honesty, consistency, material restraint and democracy, while reserving disinterested manipulation for its foreign affairs. In general the humanists of Italy accepted the political realities of the city state, at least in public,

because their patrons were the newly established ruling families. Consequently the architects and artists concerned themselves with expressing the ideal physical form of the city state, rather than proposing a new politics or a new social order. Like most things in the early Renaissance, this was a line of speculation that originated in Florence.

At the start of the fifteenth century, the Italian city states were democratic, with constitutions based on the trade guilds and allowing for rotation of office. Theoretically, any capable citizen could hold office. By 1450, however, although republicanism was nominally intact, Florence was controlled by a few wealthy families dominated by the Medici, and officials in the city were appointed by those families.

In 1435, Leone Batista Alberti, a member of a banished Florentine patrician family, returned to Florence; it was the year in which Cosimo de Medici consolidated his power. Alberti, the archetypal 'Renaissance Man' —skilled, among other things, in languages, philosophy, painting, architecture, riding, hunting and swimming—produced the first artistic treatise of the Renaissance, *On Painting.* This was followed in 1452 by *On Architecture,* an extensive treatise on the materials, techniques, forms, functions and symbolism of building, in fact 'a specification for the ideal city'. 'All I studied', he wrote, 'was how to frame the best that could possibly be, and that which deviates least from a resemblance of this, ought to be preferred above all the rest.' The ideal city of Alberti's Ten Books was to guide and provide the context for architects and city designers throughout the Renaissance. As a classical scholar, Alberti obviously thought that buildings and cities should look classical and not Gothic, but they should also be *appropriate,* in every detail, to their function, and to the social class and status of their users.

Much Renaissance architectural debate concerned the ideal form for the church, but there was no less debate on the ideal form for other sections of society, and Alberti even discussed the differences in city planning that should result if the ruler were benevolent, or a despot. 'A tyrant's fortifications must be so contrived that upon occasion he may employ the assistance of strangers against his own people and of one part of his people against the other.'

Alberti's practical model of the city is derived from Plato's *Republic.* In Book Two, he explains the 'natural' divisions of the population as described by Plato; the result in terms of building is that 'each requires a particular kind of building'.

Top: Florence under siege by the French. After the first expulsion of the Medicis in 1594, the rule of Florence and the other city states lay ultimately in the hands of France or Spain
Above: The Frontispiece of the 1513 edition of The Prince

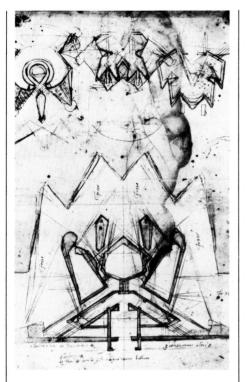

Above: Sketches for ramparts by Michelangelo. In a century constantly at war, much of the work of the Renaissance masters was on defence

Turning to the ideal Renaissance city, he again follows Plato and divides the population according to Reason, the key factor that 'separates men from brutes'.

> Select from the multitude a small number, whereof some are illustrious for their wisdom, experience and capacity; others for their knowledge in useful arts; and others, lastly, for their riches, and abundance in the goods of fortune. Who will deny that these are the most fit to be entrusted with the principle offices of the commonwealth.

Alberti believes that the state should be ruled by the intellectuals, by the artists (particularly those with skill in military engineering) and by the rich. Thus, the humanists' reading of the classics was sufficiently flexible to allow them to leave out such unfortunate aspects of Plato as communism and bring in their wealthy patrons on the trolley of Reason.

From this basic class division, the buildings of the ideal city fall into three categories: public buildings, buildings for the principle citizens and buildings for the rest. These categories are again subdivided, and different ways of building are appropriate to each group. Thus classicism was not just a new way of building, but it had a particular language which expressed the precise function of the building and the precise social position of its owner.

The city should dominate the country around, making it clear that the balance of power has shifted from the country to the city. 'Your city ought to stand in the middle of its territory, in a place from whence it can have a view all round its country,' and the city and territory should be as near as possible self-sufficient. In general, 'the commonwealth may be a defence to its subjects, an ornament to itself, a pleasure to its friends and a terror to its enemies'; it should contain room for expansion, space for 'squares, centres for chariots, gardens, places to take the air in, for swimming and the like, both for ornament and recreation'.

The public spaces and main buildings of this ideal city were beautifully illustrated in the paintings of Piero della Francesca and Francesco di Giorgio. The overall form of the ideal city was almost always polygonal, circular or star-shaped with streets radiating from the centre. This layout also had a good classical precedent in Vitruvius, who wrote the only surviving Roman treatise on architecture. Although most Roman town building, deriving as it did from military practice, used the grid-iron plan of straight streets crossing at right angles, leading to a square or rectangular city, Vitruvius favoured the radial city.

In the Renaissance this was developed with an eye to defence, and many Renaissance designers, including Giorgione and Leonardo da Vinci, were called upon to devise ramparts and city walls. Leonardo also made sketches for the rebuilding of Florence, involving the straightening of the river and its enclosure with a polygonal defensive wall. During his time in Milan, his work for Ludovico Sforza showed multilevel circulation plans that clearly illustrate the class preoccupations of the time—the highest level walkways were to be used only by the patricians and the lowest level by the plebs.

One of Ludovico's predecessors, Francesco Sforza, employed the Florentine architect Filarete, who produced a large volume of plans and drawings for an ideal city to be called Sforzinda. The plans included the Ducal palace, a cathedral, merchants' and workers' quarters and a prison. As to its shape: 'the outer walls should form a sixteen-sided figure and their height should be four times their depth. The streets should lead from the gates to the centre of the town where I would place the main square, which ought to be twice as long as it is wide. In the middle of it I would build a tower high enough to overlook the whole surrounding district.'

The centre of the ideal city poses difficult problems for the designer of a radial ideal city. All roads and views lead to it. Solutions vary from tower to temple to open space depending partly on the security of the regime—the tyrannical and therefore relatively insecure states went for the tower and its obvious use for surveillance, whereas the more secure states favoured the open square. Various fragments of the radial city were built, but the most complete was Palmonoia, a fortress town built in 1593 by Scamozzi, the last of the Renaissance architectural theorists.

The idealization of the city state continued throughout the sixteenth century not only in the work of designers such as Pietro Cataneo and Scamozzi, but also in literary works such as Francesco Patrizi's *The Happy City*, which is a recasting of Plato's *Republic* and Ludovico Zuccolo's *Evandria*.

The utopias of the Renaissance, with their emphasis on the city state and defence, reflect the political fragmentation of Christendom that had occurred since 1450, leaving a collection of competing states dominated in the Mediterranean by France and Italy. In response to the Reformation the Catholic church had launched, at the Council of Trent, a counter Reformation to attempt to reimpose Roman authority and doctrine. In the midst of these conflicts, an extraordinary Dominican monk called Tomasso Campanella began to dream of a new world order under Spanish rule. His attempts to realize this dream led to his imprisonment and torture, and it was in prison that he summed up his ideas in *City of the Sun*, one of over 100 philosophical, astrological and scientific works.

City of the Sun

Campanella was born into a poor illiterate family in Calabria, the southernmost state in Italy, in 1568. At the age of seven he was sent to a monastery and at 14 he joined the Dominican order, although he later said that he

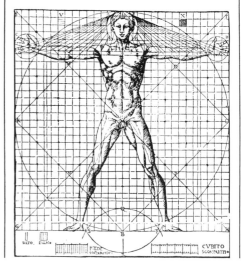

Below right: Idealized male derived from Platonic Geometry by Leonardo da Vinci
Below: Another idealized figure from Vitruvius Pollio published in 1500
Bottom: The ideal urban space for the ideal city state, by Piero della Francesca (c1420–1492)

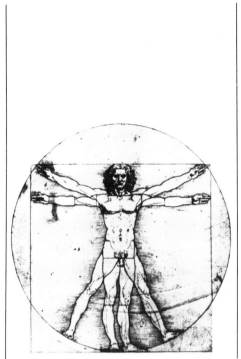

chose the monastic life for the opportunity it gave him to study rather than for religious reasons.

At 18, he left the monastery to try to visit the rationalist philosopher, Telesio, but arrived just after Telesio had died. The journey, however, brought him under the influence of the Jewish astrologer, Abraham, and Campanella became as enthusiastic an advocate of astrology and prophecy as he was of science and rationalism. In 1590, at the age of 22, he was put on trial by the Dominicans for his defence of Telesio, whose attacks on scholasticism constituted an attack on the revealed doctrines of the church.

Further charges claimed that his great knowledge was derived from communication with spirits. On this occasion he was acquitted, but three years later all his papers were stolen from a monastery in Bologna. Suspecting agents of the Papacy, he petitioned the Pope for their return, but the Pope denied all knowledge. Thirty-five years later, Campanella discovered the documents in the Papal archives. It was perhaps on the basis of these 'non-existent' documents that Campanella was accused of heresy. Although the charge was unsubstantiated, he was kept imprisoned in Rome for five years.

This was the period of the Counter-Reformation and Inquisition when the church fought back against all aspects of the Reformation and all threats to its authority. The Inquisition conducted a search-and-destroy campaign to eradicate any taint of dissent and heresy in the parts of the Christian world still under the Church of Rome. Torture was a common-place tool of interrogation and execution the equally common outcome.

When Campanella returned to Calabria in 1598, he shared the common belief that the turn of the century would bring great changes, and unusual occurrences such as floods, earthquakes or comets served as confirmation of evidence derived from the stars. But Campanella's beliefs were more specific than most. He thought the new century would bring a new Holy Universal Republic after a grand celestial conjunction in 1603. The first stage of this transformation would be to set up a Republic of Calabria, leading to an improvement in the condition of the people, to a unification of the world under the Spanish, and to a new reformation of the church.

Calabria, at the time, was under Spanish rule, so Campanella was, ironically, plotting a revolt against the local Spanish rule for the benefit of universal Spanish rule. Anyway, the plot was discovered. 140 people were arrested and taken by sea to Naples, where some of them were drawn and quartered on the deck as an example to the people of the city. They were charged with heresy and rebellion, and after the subsequent trials, ten were executed and the others imprisoned.

Campanella himself was put into solitary confinement for several months, without light and with his legs in chains. Eventually a confession was extracted from him under torture. Arrangements were made for a heresy trial, but by the time it began, in May 1600, Campanella appeared to be insane, and although the Inquisition suspected him of acting, they could not prove it, nor could they execute a mad man without damning his soul. He was sentenced to life imprisonment in 1601, and within a year had recovered enough sanity to write the first version of *City of the Sun*. Campanella was a popular figure, not only for his politics, but also for his poetry which was widely circulated in Naples during the trial, and his reputation as a wise man and magician continues in the legend that he appears in dreams to direct people to buried treasure.

City of the Sun was originally written in Italian for maximum circulation and the manuscripts smuggled out of the jail. Eventually it was published in Latin by a German publisher in 1623, although it had already received widespread circulation in several manuscript versions. The layout of Austrinopolis, the City of the Sun, reflects Campanella's interest in learning and astrology. 'It is divided into seven large rings or circles named after the seven planets, and each is connected to the next by four streets

Top: Another view of the ideal city, showing a view to be seen in many Renaissance Italian states
Above: Palmanova near Venice, one of the few concentric plans that was built, typically, as a garrison town
Above right: The site plan of Sforzinda (c1490), designed by Alberti's pupil Filarete for his patrons the Sforza family of Milan

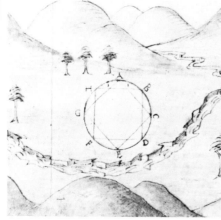

passing through four gates facing the four points of the compass.' Each circle is painted with illustrations of all the sciences so that the city itself is like a vast encyclopedia. In the third circle, for instance, 'are to be found all kinds of herbs and trees of the world, some painted on the walls, and some actually growing in baskets filled with earth . . . and there are explanations as to where they were first found, their virtues, their resemblances to the stars, metals, and parts of the human body, and their use in medicine'. The description is endless, listing metals, liquids, fishes, insects, medicines and covering geometry, geography, inventors, prophets, scientists, mechanics; and many animals including a 'real phoenix'.

In the very centre of the city, at the centre of all this knowledge as it were, is the temple 'where they honour the sun and stars as living things', especially the sun which they associate directly with God. It is 'a perfect circle, not surrounded by walls, but standing on thick columns, beautifully grouped. Its enormous dome, built with wonderful skill, has in its centre or zenith a small dome containing an opening which is right over the altar'. Two globes stand in this otherwise empty and sun-shaped altar— one showing the stars in the sky, the other showing the earth—and the stars are again reproduced on the dome above.

This temple of the stars is the home of the priests, or astrologers, who have rooms around the base of the dome.

> It is their duty to observe the stars and to note with astrolabes their movements and to know all about their effects on human affairs and their powers.

The chief priest—called Sol, O, or Metaphysic—is also the supreme ruler of the City of the Sun, assisted by three chief magistrates called Pon, Sin and Mor, which mean Power, Knowledge and Love. 'Power' looks after all matters relating to war, such as fortification, ammunition and the soldiery. 'Knowledge' controls knowledge and is responsible for all sciences, inventions and research, as well as all the materials and tools needed for them, notably the encyclopedia on the city walls. 'Love' is concerned, first of all, with reproduction. He sees to it that men and women are so mated as to produce the best offspring. Love also controls the

41

education of children, and 'medicine, pharmacy, stock raising, agriculture and everything pertaining to food, clothing and sexual intercourse.'

In the *City of the Sun*, personal love and family love have been completely replaced by love of the state. Campanella sees the family as the source of the institution of private property and does away with both: 'When men have rid themselves of selfishnesses, there remains only love for the community.'

The magistrates of reproduction select those who are to be parents after watching them exercise naked in the gymnasium, in the tradition of the Greeks. So all excesses are moderated and 'ugliness is unknown to them'. A man and a woman sleep in two separate cells until the hour of intercourse, at which time the Matron rises and opens the doors of both cells. This hour is fixed by the astrologer and the physician.

Women must be 19 and men 21 before they can be selected for breeding, but sexual activity is not entirely restricted to building the race by eugenics. 'Some are permitted access to barren or pregnant women . . . and elderly mistresses and masters provide facilities for the more passionate and stimulated ones.' This medicine is also available to any of the priests should the need arise. If romantic attachments develop, feeling must be restrained until the woman is pregnant, but such attachments are discouraged and rarely arise. Homosexuality, however, is forbidden and 'those caught committing sodomy are punished and forced to wear their shoes around their necks to show that they have perverted the natural order and as it were put their feet at their head'. Each offence is punished with greater severity, culminating in the death penalty.

Beauty, they believe, lies in 'tallness and liveliness and strength', so much so that 'if any women were to paint her face in order to make herself beautiful, or use high-heeled shoes so as to look tall, or wear lengthened garments to cover her thick legs, she would be subjected to. capital punishment'. Extreme as some of the punishments are, it must be said that Campanella, having been on the wrong end of them in the real world, has no prisons or torture in the ideal. Law, in most cases, is exercised by the leaders of particular trades.

Work in Austrinopolis, like eugenics, is regulated by science and astrology. It is considered 'noble' to be skilled at more than one trade, and the more trades the better—Metaphysic, the chief priest, is skilled in all trades and sciences. Everyone is involved in agriculture, but only the 'slow witted' work full time as farm labourers. Every corner of the country is farmed, like a garden, but they use no 'dung or filth to fertilize the fields, believing that the plants absorb some of their rottenness and make life short and weak when eaten, just as women who are beautiful from painted applications and from lack of exercise bring forth feeble offspring'. All trades, except perhaps the study of science, are considered to have equal status, but heavy work is considered particularly 'praiseworthy'. However, no one would refuse to enter a particular trade 'as their propensities are evident from their birth star, and no one does work that is harmful to him but only that which is good for him'.

Women receive the same education as men and can take up the highest occupation of scientific study, but they cannot become magistrates or leaders, although they take part in electing the lowest level of official, who are similar to the Syphogrants of Utopia. (The higher officials seem to be elected by each other.) In general, however, women take part in all the trades, but do the 'less laborious tasks'. The arrangements of communal living are intended to reduce the volume of domestic work. As in Utopia, women prepare the food and the 'young' (those under 40) serve at table.

No wages are paid, as they have no currency, but everyone receives from the storehouse what they 'deserve', as decided by the magistrates. However, everyone receives enough and the magistrates ensure that no one receives to excess:

> They claim that severe poverty makes man worthless, cunning, deceitful, thievish, contriving, vagabond, mendacious . . . and that wealth makes them insolent, proud, ignorant, traitorous, pretentious, deceptive, boastful, wanting in affection, insulting.

Below: Tommaso Campanella (1568–1639). His City of the Sun describes a society regulated by science and astrology
Bottom: Idealized male set in a magical and astrological context

Since everyone in the city works, the working day is short, only four hours; and the rest of the time is spent in personal learning, debating, reading, storytelling, writing, walking and exercising of mind and body. Again, like Utopians, they have no dice or gambling, but they also forbid any game played sitting down, including chess, and favour all energetic and sporting activities.

Socially, much of the City of the Sun is similar to the main thirty-household unit in Utopia, but, contrary to More, Campanella saw no necessity for the family. To him, the family was a positive hindrance to the strength of the state and so should disappear completely. Where More has morality Campanella has science, and while *Utopia* was an intellectual exploration, the *City of the Sun* was part of a practical campaign.

In 1629, Campanella was released from jail and went to Rome where he gained the confidence of Pope Urban IV. He had now begun to see the French as more capable of uniting the world than the Spanish and he was blamed by the latter for the pro-French policies of the Pope. In 1636 he was forced to flee to France where he taught at the Sorbonne and expounded his vision to Richelieu and Louis XIII until his death in 1639. Along with other utopian writers of the Renaissance, Campanella had prescribed an ordered society ruled from the top. But where the others had been concerned with a revival of the ideal city state, he had dreamt of a new world system dominated by an autocratic monarchy. As it was, neither of these political systems found much favour and it was the growing demand for popular democracy and power that became the major force for political and social upheaval in times to come.

Below: A sixteenth-century view of the universe. The centrepiece of the City of the Sun was a temple of the stars, which was the home of the priests or astrologers whose chief was also the supreme ruler of the city. 'It is their duty to observe the stars and their movements and to know all about their effects on human affairs and their powers'

THE
Declaration and Standard

Of the *Levellers* of *England*;
Delivered in a Speech to his Excellency the Lord Gen. *Fairfax*,
on *Friday* laft at White-Hall, by Mr. *Everard*, a late Member of the
Army, and his Prophefie in reference thereunto; fhewing what will
befall the Nobility and Gentry of this Nation, by their fubmitting to
community; With their invitation and promife unto the people, and
their proceedings in *Windfor* park, *Oatlands* park, and feverall other
places; alfo, the Examination and confeffion of the faid Mr. *Everard*
before his Excellency, the manner of his deportment with his Hat on,
and his feverall fpeeches and expreffions, when he was commanded
to put it off. Togecher with a Lift of the feverall Regiments of Horfe
and Foot that have caft Lots to go for *Ireland*.

Imprinted at *London*, for *G. Laurinfon*, Aprill 23. 1649.

'England's Spirit Unfolded'

Campanella had hoped to see his new integrated world empire founded under the authority of one of Europe's absolute monarchs. But by the time he died under the protection of the French monarch, the doctrine of the divine right of kings had come under an attack in England that resulted in the execution of the king himself. These epoch-making years of the Commonwealth saw an outbreak of republican and egalitarian utopias as well as attempts to realize the promises of the golden age and the millennium.

The Diggers

On the first day of April 1649, William Everard, Gerrard Winstanley and 15 others 'began to plant and manure the waste land upon George Hill in the County of Surrey'. Over the next few days, their numbers swelled to over 30 as they invited people from the surrounding community to join them. Everyone was to share equally in the benefits of their joint work, but, almost from the first day, the colony seems to have been harassed, and their houses, tools and crops destroyed.

Some members of the local gentry saw the 'diggers' as a threat and immediately contacted the military authorities. Within three weeks Winstanley and Everard had been summoned to appear before General Fairfax, one of Cromwell's close colleagues. On 20 April after publishing a broadsheet entitled 'The True Levellers' Standard Advanced', they travelled to London to meet him. The broadsheet declared that, 'In the beginning' no indication was ever given that one person should ever rule another. They asserted that everyone had the makings of a perfect individual who had no need for either teacher or ruler, as God was in each and every person. Moreover they believed that God was the spirit of righteousness and reason. The people had turned away from God, the inner law of righteousness, and turned towards the Serpent, which was 'covetousness branching forth into selfishness, imagination, pride, envy, hypocrisy and uncleanliness'.

In this situation, people had looked for guidance from teachers and rulers, and as a result, 'the earth which was made to be a common treasury of relief for all, both beasts and men, was hedged into enclosures by the teachers and rulers and the others were made servants and slaves . . . and the earth . . . the common storehouse for all, is bought and sold and kept in the hands of a few'. Private ownership of the land was the curse of Adam, and it had been maintained throughout Biblical and English history by theft and murder.

Besides equality of power the Diggers were also recommending a radical concept of freedom that was very different from the negative concept popularized by Locke some 40 years later. Locke said people were 'free' when there was no external constraint on their actions. In the Diggers' pamphlet, freedom is defined as equal access to resources:

> Take notice that England is not a free people till the poor that have no land have a free allowance to dig and labour the commons and so live as comfortably as the landlords that live in their enclosures . . . and that not only this common or heath should be taken in and manured by the people, but all the commons and waste ground in England and in the whole world shall be taken in by the people in righteousness, not owning any property, but taking the earth to be a common treasury,

Both rich and poor should work the land together, not as hirer and hireling but as one, and everyone was to earn their bread by the sweat of their brow, together as members of the same family. They suggest, just as Tolstoy was to do 300 years later, that the labourer should no longer work for hire, because in doing so he supported Adam's Curse. Instead, every poor person should do as they had done and begin cultivating the common. Freed from slave labour they would find what the Diggers had found—'peace in our hearts and quiet rejoicing in our work, and filled with sweet content, though we have but a dish of roots and bread for our food'.

The question of access to and ownership of the land preoccupied Winstanley in all his writings. The Diggers' Movement itself was an expression of a growing pressure from masterless men, squatters and local commoners for the means of subsistence in the land. Indeed the names 'Leveller' and 'Digger' go back to the Midland rising of 1607 against the increasing spate of enclosures.

The Diggers' platform, through Winstanley, took an optimistic view of human nature. He based his thinking on the central idea of the rationality of God within each person and in the idea that to acknowledge Christ in one's heart is to see co-operation and mutual help as natural. If people do fall into covetousness and property, then that is not necessarily inevitable or permanent, even though the individual's life may be, in the words of his contemporary Thomas Hobbes, 'nasty, brutish and short'.

Hobbes took the pessimistic view, and argued that society needed the absolute authority of a ruler to deal with the conflict that inevitably arises from a naturally competitive human nature. Winstanley, however, believed that competition resulted from the fall of Adam and was not a true characteristic of human nature. Moreover, he believed that a new age was about to dawn, in which the Holy Spirit would arise in everyone and the Law of Righteousness would prevail. In this he followed the popular myth of the millennium, in which history was divided into three ages, each dominated by one facet of the Holy Trinity. The age of the Father, the Old Testament, had already passed, and so had the age of the Son, but the age of the Spirit was about to burst forth. For Winstanley, the Third Age was not the millennialist paradise of the Apocalypse but a world ruled by rationality and co-operation.

The Puritans often regarded the Pope as the anti-Christ, the enemy of

Above: Illustrations from an anti-digger pamphlet. The diggers and other groups drew inspiration from the bible, but critics were quick to point out the folly of mere tradesmen—Winstanley was a tailor—thinking for themselves on religious matters
Above right: Supporters of the monarchy saw the English revolution as a descent into anarchy and chaos. Here, under the direction of Cromwell, the Royal Oak is being pulled down, bringing with it the other pillars of an ordered society, the Bible, the Magna Carta, and the rule of Law

God, and some regarded the whole government of the Church of England as anti-Christ too. Winstanley took the definition even further: 'Government that gives liberty to the gentry to have all the earth, and shuts out the poor commons from enjoying any part . . . is the government of imaginary self-seeking anti-Christ.' With the coming of the Third Age a ruler would become unnecessary, and the Rule of Reason, like Rousseau's idea of the General Will, would knit everyone together as upholders of the common good.

The Diggers were opposed to violence as a means of attaining the state of grace appropriate to the Third Age, for they saw co-operation and not conflict as the mark of the rule of reason. Thus, although they were subject to continuous violence, they offered no resistance, and General Fairfax seems to have been convinced, after his meeting with Winstanley and Everard, even though they refused to remove their hats in his presence, that they were a harmless group of pacifists. He visited the colony at the end of May, and was impressed by their industry and harmlessness.

The local population thought otherwise, and their crops were uprooted, tools smashed and houses torn down. In June, after a troop of soldiers had brutally beaten up some of the colonists, Winstanley wrote to Fairfax for protection, but to no avail. Fairfax probably thought that he had more pressing things to concern himself with than a group of squatters. The harassment continued, Winstanley himself was arrested and fined on two occasions, and bailiffs tried to drive away their cattle. The local lord and Member of Parliament claimed the common as his own and had several Diggers arrested for trespass, and at the end of the summer their crops were again destroyed, and their possessions burned. But the Diggers still returned and planted rye, passing the winter under cribs as they no

47

longer had the resources to build proper shelter out of wattle and daub.

In the early months of the new year, they sent out a delegation to neighbouring counties to encourage the poor to do as they had done and settle the commons. Other experiments are known to have taken place in Buckinghamshire, Hertfordshire, Middlesex, Huntingdonshire and Northamptonshire, at Coxhall, Iver, Barnet, Enfield, Dunstable and Bosworth, but it is likely that they were part of a general movement rather than the direct result of Winstanley's delegates.

The Diggers of George Hill were finally driven off at the end of March 1650, and they moved to the nearby wastes of Cobham Common. However, a week before Easter, in a remarkable display of Christian charity, Parson Platt, one of their most persistent persecutors, followed them to Cobham and with several men assaulted the men and women of the community, set fire to their new dwellings, burnt their furniture and scattered their belongings. The remaining colonists were threatened with death if they returned, and Parson Platt personally hired men to guard the common day and night to prevent any resettlement. The Digger colony had lasted nearly a year and, at its height, was cultivating about 11 acres.

Winstanley, Hobbes and Harrington

With the forced abandonment of the colony, Winstanley turned to propaganda by word rather than deed. In 1652, one year after the publication of Hobbes's *Leviathan,* which favoured absolute monarchy and private property, he published *The Law of Freedom.* His starting point, characteristically, was that every person should have the freedom to till and plant the soil, and that this freedom should be based on the common ownership of the land.

Such a proposition would have horrified James Harrington whose republican utopia *Oceana* was published four years later in 1656. In it he proposed a small-scale, property-owning democracy as the ideal basis for stable and just government. No one would be allowed to own property over the value of £2,000, but only owners of property would take part in government, whereas Winstanley would have no such limit on participation. Indeed it is likely that Harrington developed his ideas against the two polar opposites of Hobbes and the Diggers. Both Harrington and Winstanley stress the agricultural basis of their ideal societies—but while Harrington dreams of the agricultural democracy of Aristotle, Winstanley dreams of a dispersed agrarian society with craft work and no wage labour.

Commerce itself receives little attention from either, except that Winstanley bans it because it encourages the accumulation of capital and the purchase of land by merchants. In its place he substitutes a system of storehouses where the products of the land, both raw materials and finished goods, would be collected and then distributed. In the age of the Spirit every person would draw freely from the storehouse, but every able-bodied person was also required by law to engage in some useful, co-operative and productive employment and no man would be permitted to employ another.

Both Harrington and Winstanley retain a parliament and insist that representatives should serve for only one year, but Winstanley's would be chiefly involved with administrative and judicial functions, and Harrington's would be chiefly legislative. His elaborate system of government based on two chambers formed the basis of the new American Constitution 100 years later. One chamber debated, the other made decisions; there was a written constitution, decisions were reached by ballot, and selection of candidates was based on indirect election. However, qualifications were strict for these property-owning democrats. Each representative had to be a male of at least 30 years, to have undergone military service, to be married, and to own land, goods and money to a minimum value of £100.

In Winstanley's Third Age, under the rule of reason, there would be very little need of authority or parliament on the Harrington model, nor, for that matter, for the sovereign that rules in Hobbes's *Leviathan.* Both

Above: James Harrington (1611–77) whose republican utopia, Oceana, was influential in the formulation of the American Constitution

Hobbes and Harrington use the same model of the human being, the possessive individualist, and both agreed that, for that particular brand of human being, a strong government was necessary. Hobbes provided it through the absolute power of a monarch, and Harrington through a legitimate government whose authority was based on election.

Winstanley's ideas, on the other hand, made the strong state an irrelevance. When public officials were necessary they would be elected by universal manhood suffrage from candidates over 40 years old. He would involve as many people as possible in the administration of the dispersed communities and would rotate offices to eliminate any potential for personal aggrandizement that might be exploited by an entrenched official. His aim was to create a well-informed, involved and caring citizenry. After early education by their parents, all children would be sent to a school where they would 'learn to read the laws of the commonwealth and to be acquainted with all arts and languages'. All would be taught a trade, an art or a science, and be involved in productive work in the community. Winstanley explicitly stated that he would not have 'one sort of children . . . trained up only to booklearning and no other employment, called scholars'.

The writings of Winstanley, and the experiments of the Diggers and other groups lapsed into obscurity for many years, and they have only been rediscovered in this century. That later writers such as William Godwin and Thomas Spence also came up with similar ideas without any contact with the Diggers' work and history only indicates the strength of the popular tradition of an agricultural utopia. Ironically, Winstanley has often been slotted into the litany of early communists who are presented as forerunners of and justification for today's 'communism' with its centralized state, mass-production industry and violent revolutionary change. Winstanley was completely opposed to all of these.

However there were other utopian strands in the seventeenth century that do perhaps have stronger links with today's centralized industrial states, whether they are 'democratic' or 'communist'. Their roots were in the workers' republic of Johann Valentin Andreae, and in the dream of Francis Bacon that science and its application through industry might lead to untold wealth and hence to utopia.

Below: A still from the film Winstanley. 'Peace in our hearts and quiet rejoicing in our work, and filled with sweet content, though we have but a dish of roots and bread for our food.' Gerrard Winstanley

Citadels of Science

Johann Valentin Andreae, through his studies and extensive travels, became familiar with the work of radical teachers and scientists such as Comenius, Kepler and Galileo. Coming from Germany, the conflicts of the Lutheran reformation were part of his background and tradition, rather than battles to be fought through anew, as was the case with the Italian Campanella. Inevitably Andreae's travels led him to Geneva, and the place impressed him greatly, both by the 'purity of morals' of its inhabitants, and the 'absolutely free commonwealth' of its political system. He clearly felt no contradiction between the freedom of the commonwealth and the means employed by Calvin to enforce the purity of morals.

Christianopolis

Andreae, a Lutheran minister, published his *Christianopolis* at Strasbourg in 1619, some four years before *City of the Sun* appeared in print. Superficially, Christianopolis seems to be a typical Renaissance city state utopia, with its walled city, geometric layout and emphasis on religion, but it is also close to the reformist utopias of the nineteenth century. Its geometric planning is functional, not merely symbolic—work and science are closely related, and the science itself is experimental with little alchemy or astrology.

At that time, Geneva's ward supervisors, aldermen and magistrates made weekly investigations into the morals and 'even the slightest transgressions' of the Genevan citizens. There are records of capital punishment for adultery, books were systematically censored, and the weekly

Left: House for a River Surveyor, by Claude Nicolas Ledoux (1736–1806). This was one of the many special dwellings for his ideal city

sermons were compulsory. Although Andreae disapproved of the death sentence itself, he borrowed the techniques of rigorous censorship, regular and institutionalized inquisition, compulsory religious observance and severe punishment, and they became an integral part of his utopia.

Within 50 years Calvinist Geneva was to inspire another utopia, that of Gabriel de Foigney, who was to suffer so much at the hands of the regime that his utopia is a plea for moral freedom and toleration. These two utopians, in their response to Geneva, take diametrically opposing positions on 'human nature'. Andreae believed that people were innately bad, that every person carried within them 'domestic, rustic, or even paternal and inbred evil and wickedness', and that a tight moral rule was necessary to prevent everyone contaminating everyone else. De Foigney believed that people were innately good and needed no laws or rigid rule to force them to stay that way.

After joining the Lutheran ministry, Andreae moved to the cloth and dye working town of Calw where he spent his life serving its community. On top of the usual pastoral work, he started schools and eventually set up a mutual protective association for the textile workers, supported by contributions from his parishioners, which survived into this century. A concern for work and the workers is the other major influence in Andreae's utopia. He looked to the medieval city, with its guilds, ideals of brotherhood, respect for craftsmanship and protection of work and trade, and tried to preserve these both in his work and utopia.

Andreae's Christianopolis was the chief city on the island of Caphar Salama, meaning 'a place of peace', and Andreae reaches it in characteristic allegorical style, after being shipwrecked from the good ship *Fantasy*. His is the first utopia to demand an entrance examination, for, on landing, Andreae is examined by three magistrates, one to find out if he is quack, beggar or actor, the second to establish the soundness of his moral character and the third to ensure that his scientific knowledge is up to scratch.

The modest minister is eventually admitted by virtue of his cleansing ordeal by shipwreck rather than by excellence in examination. Once inside, he finds a zoned city where the ordered life of its 400 inhabitants is reflected in the geometry and symmetry of its layout. 'It's shape is a square whose side is 700 feet, well fortified with four towers and a wall. It looks, therefore, toward the four quarters of the earth.' The zones of the city depend on the type of work, with farm-based trades to the East, smelting and fire-using trades to the West, mills and bakeries to the South, and meat and supplies to the North. In each section, productive work, research, living and administration take place side by side.

Above: John Valentin Andreae (1586–1654), author of Christianopolis. He was a Lutheran Minister who was influenced by the 'purity' of Calvinistic Geneva
Top: Andreae started a school and a mutual protection association for the textile workers at the cloth-working town of Calw
Above right: Francis Bacon (1561–1626), Lord Chancellor of England and author of 'New Atlantis'

Organizationally the city is similar to the medieval guild scaled up to the level of a self-sufficient society. However, Christianopolis has no private property, no money, and no luxury. Its citizens are grouped in small nuclear families with housing and furniture provided, maintained and inspected by the city, and with food available by ration from the common store but eaten in the home. More's family was an economic unit, but Andreae's family is purely religious, with sexual relations preserved solely for reproduction: 'They have the greatest desire for conjugal chastity and they set a premium on it that they may not injure or weaken themselves by too frequent intercourse. To beget children is quite proper; but passion of licence is a disgrace.'

The aims of the community are, firstly the worship of God, secondly the cultivation of good clean morals and thirdly the development of the mental powers. Thus in education too, religion takes first place, but the educational programme is based on the latest scientific and mathematical work. Andreae wrote that, 'unless you analyse matter by experiment, unless you improve the deficiencies of knowledge by more capable instruments, you are worthless'. Science in Christianopolis was to be the 'testing of nature herself'. Astrology as well as astronomy has its place there, indeed Andreae takes it for granted, but in Christianopolis it is stripped of its occult and fatalistic aspect. It is studied 'to find how they rule the stars and by faith shake off the yoke if any exists'.

All work, especially menial work, has very high status in Christianopolis. Hours of work are short, public duties are rotated and all citizens carry arms, though unwillingly. The ample leisure time is spent in communion with God, avoiding temptation and increasing virtue. Four hundred inhabitants seems a very small number of citizens to be engaged in all this good work, but it does not include women and children. Plato, More, and Campanella all made attempts at female equality, and Andreae was certainly acquainted with the work of all three. Yet he is the first utopian, though by no means the last, to restrict women to what he considered a purely 'feminine' role. He allocates to women the weaving trades, and they receive the same basic education as the men, but they have no vote in church or council, nor control in the household. Andreae did not actually consider that this constituted any unnatural inequality, for he was following biblical precedent. Moreover, in a community that put religion and virtue first, he stressed that no virtue was inaccessible to women.

Although Christianopolis is the last of the Renaissance city states, it links science and production (and not just science and defence), and tends towards pacifism. Its work ethic and workers' organizations, and its welfare state can make it seem surprisingly similar to modern social democracies.

New Atlantis

The first basis and purpose of Christianopolis was, as its name implies, religion, and all other aspects were dependent on this higher purpose. Thus the study of nature and science, though it has high status, takes on the aspect of a religious duty. It was left to Andreae's English contemporary, Francis Bacon, to develop the theme of science. In his hands, it ceased to be a divine and academic duty, and became a tool for the domination of nature and the solution of problems in society. Knowledge, for Andreae, was for the glory of God, for Bacon, 'Knowledge is power'.

Francis Bacon, like Thomas More, was Lord Chancellor of England, but his career came to an abrupt end in 1621 when he was accused of corruption and embezzlement, fined £40,000 and sentenced to life imprisonment. However, James I, perhaps feeling that the disgrace was sufficient punishment and that Bacon had suffered enough already, relieved him of all specific punishment. Bacon retired to his country house in St Albans, to write, among other things, his utopia, *New Atlantis*, which was eventually published in 1627, one year after his death. The island of New Atlantis, or Bensalem, is the 'angelical' home of an ancient civilization, supposedly discovered by Bacon and his friends after they had been lost at sea. Behind all the utopian paraphernalia, it is an idealization of Jacobean England, complete with wealth, luxury and rank. Bensalemites have no desire or use for austerity, and Bacon never tires of describing their fine and gaudy clothing, so that he occasionally reads like a haberdasher's catalogue. Their status is unrivalled and though visitors to Bensalem are welcome guests, they are of second rank, as is made clear by the frequent hemkissings and other ritual acts of courtly deference.

New Atlantis is the incomplete fragment of a utopia. Briefly Bacon sets the context, based on the Atlantis myth in Plato's *Critias*, and describes the history of the island's constitution and religion. The constitution, an enlightened but absolute monarchy, was set up by the wise King Solamona some 1900 years before Bacon's visit. The religion is Christian, and was revealed through the convenient miracle of a sea chest containing the scriptures. This chest arrived at the island preceded by a pillar of light, and the inhabitants were so overcome by the patent truth of the contents that they promptly became converted. With almost equal brevity he describes the virtue of the people; 'You shall understand that there is not under the

Right: Setting sail for utopia! Frontispiece from a collection of Bacon's writing containing the fragments of New Atlantis

heavens so chaste a nation as this of Bensalem, nor so free from all pollution and foulness. It is the virgin of the world. . .' He stresses the importance of the family, which is paternal, with special honours given to the fathers of large families. Marriage is unbreakable, but Bacon would be more circumspect than his predecessor Thomas More on the procedures for betrothal. Instead of More's system of mutual inspection, 'they have a more civil way; for they have near every town a couple of pools (which they call Adam and Eve pools), where it is permitted to one of the friends of the man, and another of the friends of the woman, to see them severally bathe naked'.

However, Bacon's main subject is his scientific institution, Solomon's House, or the College of the Six Days Work, which has such power and authority that it is virtually a state within the state. Its aim is the study and use of science. 'The end of our Foundation is the knowledge of causes and secret motions of things, and the enlarging of the bounds of the human empire, to the effecting of all things possible.' To this end the college has seemingly unlimited resources, from vast deep caves full of instruments to half-mile high towers, complete with hermits to act as observers. Bacon throws everything in, though he describes nothing in depth— artificial lakes, wells, fountains, artificial weather chambers, medicinal baths, experimental gardens and orchards, and animal parks are all included.

> We have also divers mechanical arts which you have not, and stuffs made by them, as papers, linen, silks, tissues, dainty works of feathers of wonderful lustre, excellent dyes and many others . . . furnaces of great diversities . . . instruments also which generate heat only by motion . . . heats of dungs, and of bellies and maws of living creatures . . . perspective houses . . . sound houses, perfume houses, engine houses.

The division of scientific labour within the college, and its accompanying divisions of rank, is based on stages in the scientific process rather than areas of study such as metallurgy or biology. Thus 'Depredators' collect experiments from books, 'Mystery Men' collect them from practice, 'Pioneers' or 'Miners' conduct new experiments, 'Compilers' record the experiments, and 'Dowry Men' or 'Benefactors' analyse them. A particularly privileged group are the 'Merchants of Light'. These are the only citizens of Bensalem who are allowed to travel abroad, and they go disguised, with the express task of bringing back news of the rest of the world 'especially of the sciences, arts, manufacturers, and inventions . . . and to bring to us books, instruments and patterns of every kind'.

Here Bacon makes a decisive break with the universalist tradition of the Renaissance, with its free exchange of knowledge. Solomon's House gives nothing in return and smugly contemplates its own superiority. It protects the knowledge that is power and surrounds it with secrecy, to the extent where the Father of the House has power to withold an invention from the monarch. Bacon has made scientific knowledge the possession of the state, but it is also the possession of a privileged group within the state. Later utopians, in the first place Saint-Simon, were to propose that this group take over the whole apparatus of government.

Bacon had intended to complete *New Atlantis* with a legal framework, such as he had hoped to provide for James I, but he died before he could find the time. Later in the century, however, it was continued by two other writers, John Glanville in 1675 and an unidentified follower, R.H., in 1660. Both develop Bacon's scientific ideas, both works are justifications of monarchy and both refer to Bacon in the most illustrious terms.

Bacon's fame has continued to grow, but it has become less and less clear what is the basis of his prestige and his claim to be father of modern scientific method. Many of his scientific 'tools' already existed, and his 'method' was in use in the works of Bernard Palissey and others. Moreover, Bacon performed hardly any scientific work himself. His originality lies not in the scientific ideas themselves, but in his claim that science gave power over nature, that it could satisfy people's needs, achieve progress in

Right: An allegory of the Royal Society centred on the bust of Charles II. It was set up by Bacon's followers in 1660 for the advancement of science

society and lead to an increase in happiness. Rather than the father of scientific method, Bacon was the forefather of the modern materialistic concept of progress.

Equally important, Bacon opened the way for science to become respectable, especially in England. Before him, and for many years to come on the continent, scientific enquiry was frequently a sign of radicalism and scientists were persecuted by both church and state. Bacon, with his impeccable establishment credentials, held up the possibility that science could become a vehicle for material progress, and a tool of the state into the bargain.

However, the battle for the acceptance of science was not completed with the death of Bacon. During the Commonwealth, people in England were preoccupied with other utopian matters, and the setting up of Solomon's House had to wait until the Restoration. Eventually Bacon's followers, including John Glanville, set up the Royal Society in 1660.

Bacon's followers in France were the Encyclopedists of the eighteenth century 'Enlightenment'. They took over the task allotted to Solomon's House, the cataloguing of all knowledge to provide a rational basis for development. 'Our aim is to gather all knowledge together so that our descendants, being better instructed may become at the same time happier and more virtuous.' (Denis Diderot, *Encyclopaedie* Vol I 1751) After 8 years the *Encyclopaedie* was banned by the French Council of State, with this verdict: 'The advantages to be derived from a work of this sort, in respect to progress in the arts and sciences, can never compensate for the irreparable damage that results from it in regard to morality and religion.'

The Enlightenment belief in progress was attacked by Rousseau who was a contributor to the *Encyclopaedie* and a friend of Diderot, the

editor. He saw science as bringing moral ruin, abundance as a breeder of luxury and corruption, and progress as an illusion, with 'society' as merely a corruption of an original ideal state of nature.

From Geneva to the State of Nature

Many of the ideas of the Enlightenment had been anticipated during the previous century in the utopia of Gabriel de Foigney. Given the official French response to the Encyclopedists, it is hardly surprising that, 70 years earlier, the work of de Foigney failed to please the authorities in Geneva.

Gabriel de Foigney was born in France, grew up as a Roman Catholic, entered the Order of Cordeliers and became a preacher. Before long, his 'scandalous behaviour' led to his being expelled and defrocked, leaving him both homeless and in poverty. He went to Geneva where he managed to convince the authorities that he had made a genuine change of faith, and was allowed to settle in the city. Here he began to rebuild his reputation, with several seductions of servant girls, a broken promise of marriage, and an engagement to a disreputable widow, whom he later married. Expelled from Geneva, he went first to Lausanne, and then to Berne, where he eventually found a job as a minister in the College of Morges.

All went quietly until he wrote a work on the divine service which was considered to contain papist deviations. Attempts were made to dismiss him, and, characteristically, de Foigney soon provided the opportunity by conducting divine service while drunk and vomiting in front of the communion table. Surprisingly, he was readmitted to Geneva, where he attempted to regain his credibility with an edition of the psalms. This was all to no avail, for papist deviations were again detected and the edition was confiscated and destroyed.

At this point he seems to have given up hope of ever pleasing the authorities and in 1676 published his utopia, *The Adventures of James Sadeur and the Discovery of Australia.* Two professors in the Academy of Geneva considered it 'full of extravagances, falsehoods and even dangerous, infamous and blasphemous things'. He was imprisoned and released on bail, but the charges were never carried through. Genevan law was no longer administered with the rigour that had so impressed Andreae, and de Foigney had suceeded in finding friends amongst the magistrates.

He caused offence firstly in his attitude to religion, for he denied the relevance or possibility of any revelation, explaining that for God to reveal himself to one group of people and not another would be an injustice. His Australians assume that some kind of incomprehensible god exists, but they don't like to mention him: 'their religion is not to speak of religion'. Without churches, ministers, doctrines, congregations or services, de Foigney's religion becomes plain deism.

The inhabitants' reticence extends also to the mention of sex, though the common form of greeting was the kissing of hands 'and the private parts'. They are described as red skinned with black hair, standing 8 feet tall with long faces. They have 12 fingers and 12 toes and are accustomed to go naked, explaining that if nature meant them to have clothes they would have been given them.

De Foigney argued that all dispute arose from differences, of whatever sort. Thus his Australians are of one sex and go naked to avoid the distinctions which clothes create. Australians make a profession of absolute equality, with an ethic of equal 'brotherhood' and equal education (a school-leaving age of 35 years). The climate has no seasons, and there is no government. 'Our glory consists in being all alike.'

Curiously, de Foigney in his utopia combines devotion to study and skill in scientific research and invention, with the ancient concept of the fruitful land. The Australians do little physical work and experience no pain, so they have little need for the many inventions that they make, merely to be recorded in their *Book of Public Curiosities.* In his Australia, scientific study is conducted for its own sake, in contrast to Andreae who would do it for God, and Bacon who would do it for the state.

As well as offending Genevan concepts of religion, and satirizing their attitude to sex, de Foigney was no less radical in his concept of human nature. 'It was the Nature of Man', he wrote, 'to be born, and live free, and he could not be subjected without being despoiled of his nature'.

It is a small step to the words of de Foigney's fellow Genevan, Rousseau: 'Man was born free, and he is everywhere in chains.' However, this may well be where comparison ends, for Rousseau, like Andreae, saw much good in Geneva, mainly because of its democratic constitution.

Symbols of the Revolution

Despite the radical speculations of Rousseau and the Encyclopedists, the hundred years leading up to the French Revolution produced few traditional literary utopias, though the tradition did not die out completely. L. S. Mercier won the remarkable distinction of living to be part of the revolution in France that he had forecast in his utopia, *Memoirs of the Year 2500.* Forced to flee France after the book's publication in 1770, he eventually returned to become a member of the National Assembly. Later imprisoned by Robespierre, he survived to become an enthusiastic supporter of Napoleon. His critics observed that 'Mercier, having been a republican under the monarchy, ought to be permitted to become a royalist under the republic'. Despite Mercier's apparent 'flexibility', he always claimed to be a staunch republican.

A more influential utopian work of the time was Morelly's *Code of Nature,* one of the earliest expressions of French communism. Within a couple of years of its publication in 1775 it was known throughout Europe. The final chapter describes an ideal society in which labour has been made attractive, private property abolished and education is compulsory and free. Morelly does not seem to rate marriage too highly; in Mercier's third

Top: L. S. Mercier, whose memoirs of the year 2500 forecast the French Revolution
Above: The title page of Abbé Morelly's Code of Nature, an early and influential expression of French communism
Right: A celebration of the French Revolution, with Rousseau, the tricolour and the cap of Liberty

58

millennium it is compulsory for men, but celibacy is allowed after the age of 40. Morelly believed, with de Foigney, that people were naturally good, but also that it was secondary environmental factors that created evil. He proposed a society 'in which the idea of good and evil itself was abolished'. His underlying principle, pre-dating the communist movement by 100 years, was that 'each is to labour according to his ability and receive according to his needs'.

Other utopian fragments exist in the work of the Marquis de Sade and of Babeuf who advocated equality in everything, the first emphasizing individual freedom, and the second a rigorous equality – 'the aim of society is the happiness of all, and happiness consists in equality'. But for the most part the traditional utopian devices were pointless, and even counterproductive, to writers who believed that society itself could be changed, and who were involved in making those changes. However, the gap was more than filled by the utopian projects of the architects Boullée and Ledoux who expressed the ideas of their age with extraordinary force.

Boullée's most stunning project, the Cenotaph for Newton, is the consummate monument to the belief in progress through science. Today it is easy to take Newton for granted, but for the eighteenth century his work was the proof that science could and would understand 'the causes and secret motions of things' and would lead to 'the effecting of all things possible'. Newton, it seemed, had given substance to Bacon's profession of faith in science as the tool of progress. Boullée's design places the tomb at the base of a vast and otherwise empty sphere, pierced with openings to give the effect of a starlit sky.

The use of simple unadorned geometry was characteristic of the work of both Boullée and Ledoux. They rejected all superfluous ornament or historical precedent, for these expressed the traditions of the old order. They wished their own designs to be dictated by reason and nature, but by 'nature' they did not mean a romantic naturalism, with the copying of

natural forms, rather the idea that everything had a particular nature of its own. For instance, in his National Assembly project, Boullée tried to express the ideas of democracy and human rights in a form that was 'natural', or appropriate, to those ideas. It would not have been appropriate to base the design on a leaf structure and plaster the surface with acanthus leaves, but it was appropriate to base the designs on pure, simple squares, circles, cubes and spheres. Thus the projects have a geometrical simplicity expressed by the basic Platonic solids which were felt to be appropriate to the universal and eternal truth of the concepts with which they were dealing.

Above: Boullée's design for a lighthouse, another example of the range of the revolutionary architect's interests
Right: Interior of the Newton Cenotaph: 'I wanted to give Newton that immortal resting place, the Heavens'

Boullée's work was more concerned with the ideals of the Enlightenment, but Ledoux's projects are models for the future. Until the revolution, Ledoux had been Inspector of the Royal Saltworks where he was required to design and build offices, factory building and housing. But Ledoux considered that the architect should be 'rival to the creator', and concerned himself with all aspects of the community, from work, morals and education to legislation, culture and government. The utopian writers had always included architectural descriptions in their work, but Ledoux was the first architect to turn utopian, beginning a tradition of speculation that continues today. When he interpreted his employment at the Saltworks

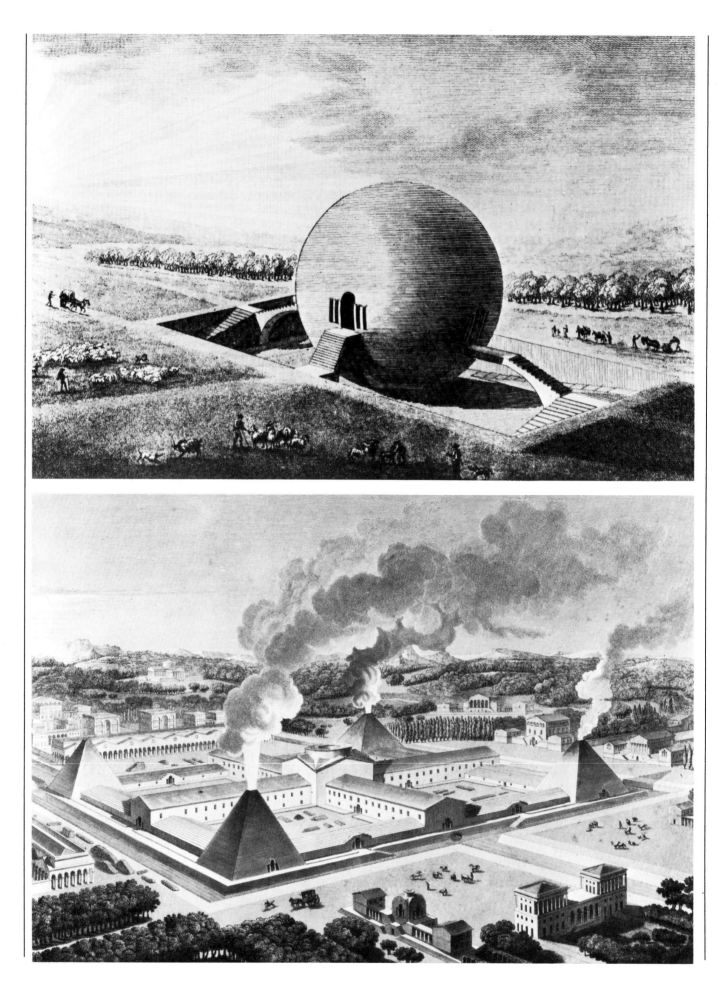

as a commission to design an ideal city, his first project was rejected by Louis XV as the 'product of mania'.

He continued to work on the idea and various versions appear in the book on architecture that he was working on when he died in 1806. The final Chaux is a garden city for an ideal community, but designed for an actual rather than a mythical site. Loosely linked to the overall plan are many designs for particular buildings to suit the inhabitants of the new age. Instead of palaces for princes and aristocrats, Ledoux designed houses for lumbermen, engineers, brokers, writers, art dealers, surveyors and charcoal burners.

In place of the aggrandizement of royalty, he projected a heroic context for the newly liberated citizens. Temples are dedicated to Justice and Happiness, and a Union House, designed as a meeting place and club-house, expresses the ideal of fraternity. The Oikema, House of Passion, or Temple of Immorality, is an educational building in which young people were to be exposed to concentrations of vice so that they would be repelled in the direction of virtue. A typical architectural utopian, Ledoux explores few of the social implications of his symbols and does not explain how the therapists are to be recruited for his aversion centre. Other projects, inspired by Rousseau and his recommendation of the rural life, show country communes. In these sheltered retreats, people can escape the sophistications and corruption of the city and live 'natural' lives surrounded by orchards, vineyards and fields.

Revolutionary periods inspire great projects, but they are not periods when buildings get built. When eventually the situation in France became more stable and building restarted, architecture took on an aggrandizing role similar to its role before the revolution. The only difference was in the style. Ledoux and Boullée had not been concerned with the surface decoration of their façades but with content, with new types of building, new users and new ideals. They had no more success in building their designs under the new order than they had had under the old.

Left: 'A shelter for the rural guards', projected by Ledoux. Its pure geometry is typical of his designs
Below left: Ledoux's design for the Royal Saltworks, where he was architect and surveyor for 20 years before the revolution
Below: The central market area of his ideal city of Chaux. It was accompanied with detailed site plans and many designs for houses and special buildings

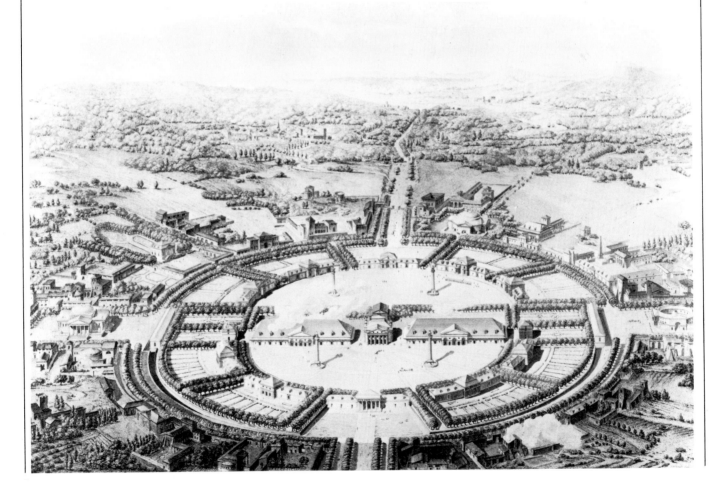

DÉCLARATION DES DROITS DE L'HOMME ET DU CITOYEN.

Décretés par l'Assemblée Nationale dans les séances des 20, 21, 23, 24 et 26 août 1789, acceptés par le Roi.

PRÉAMBULE

LES représentans du peuple François, constitués en assemblée nationale, considérant que l'ignorance, l'oubli ou le mépris des droits de l'homme sont les seules causes des malheurs publics et de la corruption des gouvernemens, ont résolu d'exposer dans une déclaration solennelle, les droits naturels, inaliénables et sacrés de l'homme, afin que cette déclaration, constamment présente à tous les membres du corps social, leur rappelle sans cesse leurs droits et leurs devoirs, afin que les actes du pouvoir legislatif et ceux du pouvoir exécutif, pouvant être à chaque instant comparés avec le but de toute institution politique, en soient plus respectés; afin que les reclamations des citoyens, fondées désormais sur des principes simples et incontestables, tournent toujours au maintien de la constitution et du bonheur de tous.

EN conséquence, l'assemblée nationale reconnoit et déclare, en presence et sous les auspices de l'Etre suprème les droits suivans de l'homme et du citoyen.

ARTICLE PREMIER.

LES hommes naissent et demeurent libres et égaux en droits, les distinctions sociales ne peuvent être fondées que sur l'utilité commune.

II.

LE but de toute association politique est la conservation des droits naturels et imprescriptibles de l'homme; ces droits sont la liberté, la proprieté, la sureté, et la résistance à l'oppression.

III.

LE principe de toute souveraineté réside essentiellement dans la nation, nul corps, nul individu ne peut exercer d'autorité qui n'en émane expressement.

IV.

LA liberté consiste a pouvoir faire tout ce qui ne nuit pas à autrui Ainsi, l'exercice des droits naturels de chaque homme, n'a de bornes que celles qui assurent aux autres membres de la société la jouissance de ces mêmes droits; ces bornes ne peuvent être déterminées que par la loi.

V.

LA loi n'a le droit de défendre que les actions nuisibles à la société. Tout ce qui n'est pas défendu par la loi ne peut être empêché, et nul ne peut être contraint à faire ce qu'elle n'ordonne pas.

VI.

LA loi est l'expression de la volonté générale; tous les citoyens ont droit de concourir personnellement, ou par leurs représentans, à sa formation; elle doit être la même pour tous, soit qu'elle protege, soit qu'elle punisse. Tous les citoyens étant égaux à ses yeux, sont également admissibles a toutes dignités, places et emplois publics, selon leur capacité, et sans autres distinction que celles de leurs vertus et de leurs talens.

VII.

NUL homme ne peut être accusé, arrêté, ni détenu que dans les cas déterminés par la loi, et selon les formes qu'elle a prescrites, ceux qui sollicitent, expédient, exécutent ou font exécuter des ordres arbinaires, doivent être punis; mais tout citoyen appelé ou saisi en vertu de la loi, doit obéir a l'instant, il se rend coupable par la résistance.

VIII.

LA loi ne doit établir que des peines strictement et évidemment nécessaire, et nul ne peut être puni qu'en vertu d'une loi établie, et promulguée antérieurement au délit, et légalement appliquée.

IX.

TOUT homme étant présumé innocent jusqu'à ce qu'il ait été déclaré coupable, s'il est jugé indispensable de l'arrêter, toute rigueur qui ne serait pas nécessaire pour s'assurer de sa personne doit être sévèrement réprimée par la loi.

X.

NUL ne doit être inquiété pour ses opinions, mêmes religieuses pourvu que leur manifestation ne trouble pas l'ordre public établi par la loi.

XI.

LA libre communication des pensées et des opinions est un des droits les plus precieux de l'homme; tout citoyen peut donc parler, écrire, imprimer librement, sauf à répondre de l'abus de cette liberté dans les cas déterminés par la loi.

XII.

LA garantie des droits de l'homme et du citoyen nécessite une force publique: cette force est donc instituée pour l'avantage de tous, et non pour l'utilité particuliere de ceux a qui elle est confiée.

XIII.

POUR l'entretien de la force publique, et pour les dépenses d'administration, une contribution commune est indispensable; elle doit être également répartie entre les citoyens en raison de leurs facultées.

XIV.

LES citoyens ont le droit de constater par eux même ou par leurs représentans, la nécessité de la contribution publique, de la consentir librement, d'en suivre l'emploi, et d'en déterminer la quotité, l'assiette, le recouvrement et la durée.

XV.

LA société a le droit de demander compte a tout agent public de son administration.

XVI.

TOUTE société, dans laquelle la garantie des droits n'est pas assurée, ni les séparation des pouvoirs déterminée, n'a point de constitution.

XVII.

LES propriétés étant un droit inviolable et sacré, nul ne peut en être privé, si ce n'est lorsque la nécessité publique, légalement constatée, l'exige évidemment, et sous la condition d'une juste et préalable indemnité.

AUX REPRESENTANS DU PEUPLE FRANCOIS

The Land is the People's Farm

The French Revolution, like the English Revolution before it, produced a ferment of radical thinking and debate that stirred the whole of society. To writers as different as Burke, Paine, Spence and Godwin, it acted as an intense catalyst and, inspired by its example, all of them produced their major works within a period of five years.

William Godwin wrote *An Enquiry Concerning Political Justice* in 1793 as a comprehensive answer to Edmund Burke's *Reflections on the Revolution in France.* Like many philosophical conservatives since his day, Burke saw politics as a matter of expediency and not of theoretical ideas. He based his judgement on experience, not theory, and experience told him that democracy would lead to tyranny. His attack was upon the democratic theories of the French revolution and the possible spread of these ideas to England.

The democratic tyranny Burke discussed is now associated with 'public opinion'. 'Those who are subjected to wrong under multitudes', he wrote, 'are deprived of all external consolation. They seem deserted by mankind, overpowered by a conspiracy of their whole species.' This observation is particularly apt when applied to Godwin and other writers who stress public opinion or mutual censorship as the agent of control in their utopias.

Although Burke's *Reflections* may have been the immediate stimulus for Godwin to write his enquiry *Concerning Political Justice,* and the French Revolution may have provided the climate in which to do so, the central ideas of his work owe a great deal to his dissenting upbringing. From the age of 11 he was the only pupil of the pastor of the Independence Congregation in Norwich. This pastor was a disciple of Robert Sandeman whose small sect was expelled from the Presbyterian Church for denying any form of church government.

Top: William Godwin (1756–1836), author of Political Justice in which he advocated a system of independent parishes with no central government
Above: A contemporary English caricature of the French Revolution, which served to discredit home-grown preachers of liberty such as Godwin, Spence and Paine

Although from about the age of 25 Godwin began slowly to reject his religious upbringing, he never really got beyond secularizing the non-conformist's religious view of the world. The Sandemanians rejected church government; Godwin rejected any form of government. The Independent Church established separate congregations with no formal leadership; Godwin wanted a network of independent parishes without government. In secularizing the radical part of the dissenting tradition, he changed the purpose of life from being a preparation for a heavenly kingdom to the realization of heaven on earth.

In *Political Justice,* published in February 1793, he started with the belief that society originated in the need for mutual assistance and that its guiding moral principle was justice. The best social environment in which this mutual assistance could take place, he thought, was one characterized by decentralization and simplification. He dissolved the state into a local administration based on parishes and, just as Winstanley proposed for local administration, distributed the workload as widely as possible. People, he believed, were not innately bad or authoritarian, but were shaped that way by social circumstances. The need for force in past societies came not from human nature, but from institutions which corrupt people. If these institutions were removed, people would grow to be ruled by justice and wisdom, and the distinction between the common and the individual's interest would become blurred, if not disappear.

Under the rule of justice, everyone by the nature of reason becomes compelled to do everything possible for each other, and the common good is therefore realized. In order to abolish coercion between people, it would be necessary to place property on an equitable basis. But if everyone is able to claim an equitable share of the common property, he also has a duty to an equal share of the tasks that create the common well-being.

> Justice directs that each man, unless perhaps he be employed more beneficially to the public, should contribute to the cultivation of the common harvest of which each man consumes a share. This reciprocity . . . is of the very essence of justice.

Godwin's agrarian arcadia is very similar to Winstanley's 100 years before him and those of Morris or Kropotkin 100 years later. Their vision is that of people working together in the fields and workshops, and then taking from a common warehouse according to their needs. All stressed that work is happiness and envisaged a dramatic simplification of life.

The popularity of *Political Justice* was immediate but short-lived. Godwin's disciples included Wordsworth, Coleridge and Southey, but in the dark days at the end of the century, one by one they deserted him. Shelley was probably Godwin's most faithful disciple, and through his verse he transmitted the spirit of Godwin to a much wider public.

The Hive of Liberty

Before he wrote his book on Political Justice, William Godwin had been involved in the committee set up to publish the most important book of the day, *The Rights of Man* by Tom Paine. Paine began with a defence of the principles of the French revolution, but his book gradually evolved into an analysis of arbitrary government, poverty, war and unemployment. He advocated republicanism, with the state providing universal education, poor relief, old age pensions and public works, all of which would be financed by progressive income tax.

It has often been said that Paine's ideas were followed to their logical conclusions in the work of Thomas Spence. His publications were part of the climate of Jacobin and radical London and they provided the backdrop for the emergence of Owenism and Chartism after the Napoleonic Wars. Born in Newcastle-upon-Tyne in 1750 of Scottish parents, Spence, like William Godwin, owes key elements of his thought to his non-conformist background. His education consisted in his father teaching him to read the Bible—often while he worked—and making his sons stand by him reading to themselves. He would later question them on what they had learnt. The family attended the chapel of a Presbyterian minister, the Reverend J. Murray, who had not been ordained, since he believed in the congregational system of church government. Murray was to remain one of Spence's close friends until Murray's death in 1782. The influence of non-conformism can also be seen in Spence's friend and brother, Jeremiah, who was a member of the Glassites, a dissenting sect which advocated republican equality, ate together on every Sabbath and practised a community of goods.

Another close friend of Spence's during his early years in Newcastle was the woodcutter, engraver and printer, Thomas Bewick. Bewick called Spence 'one of the warmest philanthropists in the world'. They first met in the workshops of Grey's bookbinders in Newcastle, and it was Bewick who cut the steel punches for Spence's phonetic alphabet which was published in 1775, the year of the American War of Independence. In that same year, a debating society was formed in Newcastle called the Philosophical Society and both Murray and Spence joined. On 8 November Spence read a paper to the society which was the first version of his agrarian plan. Like Hobbes, Locke and Rousseau before him, he began his treatise with a description and definition of a state of nature, which was a common way of grounding theory in self-evident truths.

His starting point was the natural and equal rights of everyone to access to land, just as they have air, light or heat from the sun. The contemporary structure of ownership arose, he stated, when 'the land with all its appurtenances' was claimed by a few. This 'usurpation' went unquestioned

Above: This half-penny token by Thomas Spence (1750–1814) shows The Three Thomases, noted advocates of the Rights of Man
Below: Spence used the popular story of Robinson Crusoe as a vehicle for his utopia

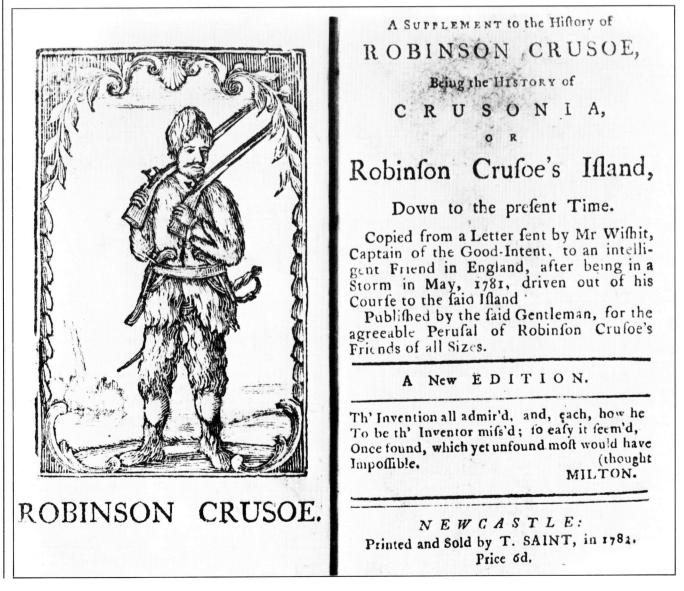

ROBINSON CRUSOE.

A SUPPLEMENT to the History of

ROBINSON CRUSOE,

Being the HISTORY of

CRUSONIA,

OR

Robinson Crusoe's Island,

Down to the present Time.

Copied from a Letter sent by Mr Wishit, Captain of the Good-Intent, to an intelligent Friend in England, after being in a Storm in May, 1781, driven out of his Course to the said Island

Published by the said Gentleman, for the agreeable Perusal of Robinson Crusoe's Friends of all Sizes.

A New EDITION.

Th' Invention all admir'd, and, each, how he
To be th' Inventor miss'd; so easy it seem'd,
Once found, which yet unfound most would have
Impossible.   (thought
                              MILTON.

NEWCASTLE:
Printed and Sold by T. SAINT, in 1782.
Price 6d.

*Top: An enthusiastic crowd raise the cap of liberty during the French Revolution
Above: In England Spence repeats the gesture, but with the head of the Prime Minister, William Pitt, on a pole*

and people fell into a habit of thinking, and of acting, as if the earth was made for them, and did not scruple to call it their property, 'which they might dispose of without regard to any other living creature in the universe'. 'No one was able now except in fear of his life to claim a sight to so much as a blade of grass, a nut, an acorn without permission.' Spence proposed that the natural state be reasserted.

Reason dictated, Spence thought, that every man should have an equal share in land. A day was therefore to be appointed when all the inhabitants of each parish would meet to take possession of their natural rights. Each parish would become a democratic corporation possessing all the land and the buildings within its boundaries. The parish would be the sole landlord, having all the normal powers and responsibilities of ownership except the right of sale. The only landlords would be the parishes, each of them having sovereign powers over its area. The land was to be divided and 'let in small farms', the rent from which went for poor relief, officers' pay, repairing buildings and keeping a magazine of ammunition.

Spence believed that the commitment of each citizen to his corporation would make the political structure very durable and that by example it would convert new nations. On the advice of the Reverend Murray, Spence published his lecture and sold it on the street for one half-penny. But he published it as an essay read to the Philosophical Society, and for using the society's name and for the 'ignoble mode of circulation', Spence was expelled from the society. Murray defended his friend at ensuing meetings, but to no avail.

Spence's next publication is in the tradition of some of the first utopian writers, in that it is a discussion of an imaginary island. He published his *History of Crusonia on Robinson Crusoe's Island* in 1782, and it is probable that the illustration of Robinson Crusoe was cut by Bewick. In principle, Crusonia differs very little from the society he outlined in his Newcastle lecture, only the setting is different. The inhabitants developed their constitution after Robinson Crusoe had left the island on which he was marooned. The reporter is a sea captain who at first is very sceptical of any society based on very local administration, small farms and no private ownership, but who comes to admire the island the inhabitants have created as he discourses with his host. 'Instead of Anarchy, Idleness, Poverty and Meanness, the natural consequences, as I narrowly thought, of a ridiculous levelling scheme, nothing but Order, Industry, Wealth and most pleasing Magnificence!' He describes the island's topography, like 'an infinite number of real gardens', words echoed 12 years later in his description of the Island of Spensonia.

In both Crusonia and Spensonia he fills out the details of his original plan. In terms of political structures, he advocates complete adult male and female suffrage electing paid members. The parish was to provide public baths, granaries, hospitals, education and libraries. Above all, in his descriptions of the imaginary islands, Spence attempts to demonstrate a society more rationally organized to serve the needs of the whole of mankind.

Spence moved to London in 1792 two years before publishing *Spensonia.* He opened a small bookshop in Chancery Lane selling his own publications and similar republican tracts. In February 1793, he was arrested for selling Thomas Paine's *Rights of Man,* but was never prosecuted. In May 1794 he was arrested again, this time on suspicion of high treason, and committed to Newgate Prison where he remained without trial until his discharge on 22 December. By 1795 he had been arrested four times since his arrival in London. Early in 1794 he opened his shop 'The Hive of Liberty' at No 8, Little Turnstile, Holborn, where he ran a small publishing business and numismatists' shop. He published his own works, including the broadsheet *Pig's Meat,* and had his own tokens stamped for sale at his shop.

In April 1798 he was again arrested for publishing *Pig's Meat,* but charges were not pressed and he returned to his business. His next arrest was in 1801 for publishing a 'seditious libel'—*The Restorer of Society to*

Above: This token provided publicity for Spence's journal Pig's Meat, *with the emblems of church and state under trotter and the cap of liberty above*
Left: A selection of Spence political tokens showing, from the left: Cain and Abel—the beginning of oppression; the destruction of title deeds to land and the end of oppression; the fate of the radical before the revolution; and the final freedom under the tree of liberty after the revolution

Its Natural State, and for this he was at last found guilty and sentenced to a fine of £20 and one year in prison. Upon his release he returned to his business as a bookseller and published *The Trial,* which contained the whole work that had led to his imprisonment. Very little is known of his life in the following years, except that he remained an itinerant bookseller. A society of Spenceans was formed during the first years after his imprisonment and the membership seems to have increased and decreased with the times.

Spence and his disciples adopted any possible way to get their ideas into circulation. In 1812, for instance, during the unrest associated with the Luddites, Lord Sidmouth wrote to the police calling attention to the street literature and to the chalking of 'improper inscriptions' such as 'Spence's Plan and Full Bellies' on walls and buildings.

Spence died in 1814, leaving to his friends just an imperative 'to promote the plan and remembrance of his inflexible integrity'. After his death, Thomas Evans, one of Spence's most ardent and unswerving disciples,

Below: This woodcut by Thomas Bewick (1753–1828) illustrated Oliver Goldsmith's poem The Deserted Village: 'But a bold peasantry, their country's pride, When once destroyed, can never be supplied'

remodelled the society into the Spencean Philanthropists. Its aim and methods, and 'Spence's Plan' are described in one of its handbills:

> For parochial Partnerships in the land
> Is the only effectual remedy for the
> Distresses and oppression of the People.
> The Landholders are not Proprietors in chief, they are but
> stewards of the Public
> For the land is the People's Farm.

In February 1817, the Committee of Secrecy reported that the Spencean societies had multiplied among mechanics, manufacturers, discharged soldiers and sailors. A little later that year, an Act of Parliament selected the Spenceans for special attention: 'all societies and clubs calling themselves Spencean or Spencean Philanthropists . . . shall be utterly suppressed and prohibited as being unlawful combinations and conspiracies against the government of our Sovereign Lord the King'.

A little before the passing of this act Evans and his son had been arrested. They were not released until 28 July 1817, by which time their case had reached most of the important newspapers and periodicals. Spence and his followers were clearly notorious and it would have been impossible to be in London in between 1812 and 1820 without knowing of the Spenceans. So it is strange that Robert Owen, the crusading industrial philanthropist turned utopian, failed to acknowledge any debt to their scheme. His similarity to these radical political reformers is, at times, almost uncanny, yet Owen has been described as having 'a vacant place in his mind where most men have political responses'. He was able successfully, whether by design or through innocence, to skirt over the issues of ownership which Evans attacked head on. This would explain why, when Evans was being roughly treated in jail, Lord Sidmouth was discussing the proposals of the 'enlightened Mr Owen'.

Top: The freeborn Englishman, manacled and deprived of free speech by the 'Gagging' Act of 1795
Above: On the reverse side of this token, utopia, with the shepherd minding his flock in peace and freedom

William Cobbett – Freeborn Englishman

Despite the attempts of Spence and his followers to contact a wider readership through the journal *Pig's Meat*, Spence seems to have had little influence outside the radical coterie that developed in London after 1790. Their writings had small impact on the urban or rural populations. Possibly the style of analysis was premature during the first years of the industrial revolution, when the nature of the society that was being created was still very indistinct. Certainly William Cobbett adopted a different style and sought a different relationship with his readers and audience.

However, Cobbett and Spence are not completely at odds. A similar dissenting background can be traced in Cobbett's childhood, when he 'most firmly believed . . . that the Pope was a prodigious woman, dressed in a dreadful robe, which had been made red by being dipped in the blood of Protestants'. But he seems to have been much more open and willing to learn from the population. This is the key to Cobbett's success, for he was able to reflect the mood of his times quite accurately and appeal to the sense of injustice and nostalgia that can create a popular utopianism.

His analysis of the agrarian situation was very similar to that made by Winstanley and the Diggers, for they saw the growth of the commercial system as the great enemy. He echoes Thomas More, Winstanley and even Oliver Goldsmith when he says:

> The taxing and funding . . . system has . . . drawn the real property of the nation into fewer hands; it has made land and agriculture objects of speculation; it has, in every part of the Kingdom, moulded many farms into one; it has almost entirely extinguished the race of small farmers, from one end of England to the other, the houses which formerly contained little farmers and their happy families are now seen sinking into ruins . . .

The enclosure movement during the period 1750 to 1850 converted some six million acres (a quarter of the country's cultivated area) from open field, common land, meadow or waste into private fields. It destroyed 'the scratch as scratch can' subsistence economy of the poor, and the cottager without any title to his land was very rarely compensated. Enclosure, as the social historian E. P. Thompson concludes, was a 'plain enough case of class robbery, played according to fair rules of property'.

Enclosure involved the imposition on the village community of alien capitalist property definitions and attacked customary rights of gleaning, access to fuel and tethering of stock. It was the final friction at the end of a long process of attrition on the customary relations of the rural community; the consolidation of commercial agriculture was ruinous for the cottager who had always been immensely vulnerable because he could rarely be totally self-sufficient. The simultaneous proliferation of factories with their mass production meant that he could no longer rely on selling goods that he manufactured to augment his income during his slack periods. He was increasingly thrown from temporary to total support by wage labour. This same process was taking place amongst the independent producers of textiles in the north, where the factory system was beginning to displace the outworkers. In both situations the aim was the increased predictability of the machine.

Right: A contemporary cartoon entitled 'The state of the country'. From 1831 to 1834 the 'Captain Swing' campaigns by the agricultural workers opposed the introduction of threshing machines and the high level of church tithes

It was against the reduction of all working relationships to the wage that William Cobbett reacted in the first two decades of the nineteenth century, and in his reaction he was echoing the feelings of many a rural labourer and cottage manufacturer.

Cobbett, as Thompson says, was the 'freeborn Englishman incarnate'. His outlook was very similar to that of the small producers. The values which he endorsed were those of sturdy individualism and independence. He mourned the disappearance of the small farmer, tradesman and weaver and in this he no doubt reflected an emerging mythology of a previous golden age of the independent producer.

Spence would have no doubt retorted that Cobbett was fooling himself and others. In his *Restorer of Society to Its Natural State* (1800), Spence had written:

> It is childish to expect ever to see small farms again, or ever to see anything else than almost screwing and grinding of the poor, till you quite overturn the present system of landed property. For they have got more completely into the spirit and power of oppression now than was ever known before.

Spence's fundamental analysis, however, was mistaken. The source of the actual agricultural discontent of the time was principally economic. The agricultural labourer was not without spirit, he had many ways of evening the score with his employer before the spread of effective police forces during the 1850s and frequently resorted to them. And if there was a vision motivating these acts of burning, smashing and stealing then it was that they were a recompense for the disappearance of the customary rights of the freeborn Englishman.

Despite their protests, the course of the industrial revolution was inexorable and many were forced off the land. The rural labourers that moved to the towns took Cobbett's vision of rural independence with them. The experience of unemployment and the squalor of towns in the 1840s nurtured the longing for access to land into a potent part of working-class culture. So ironically the agricultural utopia became the dream of the urban labourer. The most potent expression of this image of an embryonic utopia was realized in the Chartist Land Company. At its height the company had 70,000 subscribers, a share issue in excess of £90,000 and more than 600 branches throughout the country, staggering statistics for a working-class organization in the mid-nineteenth century.

Although its support depended on the dream of rural independence and self sufficiency, the company's phenomenal success during 1847 was based on the writing and oratory of Fergus O'Connor. O'Connor was born in County Cork sometime around 1796 of a family that claimed to be of Irish royal descent, and was brought up with both aristocratic aims and radical ideas. In 1820 he inherited an estate and seems to have busied himself with its affairs. In addition he studied the law in Dublin, was called to the bar, joined the local Whigs, and in 1832 was elected as an MP for County Cork. It was this that brought him to London.

In 1834, however, it was discovered that his estate was not his own freehold property and therefore he was disqualified as an MP. He stayed in England and became involved with the London Working Men's Association. In 1838, the Association drew up a six-point charter for: the payment of Members of Parliament, annual elections, universal manhood suffrage, vote by secret ballot, abolition of property qualifications and equal electoral districts. However, the Chartist leaders soon became afraid that O'Connor's inflammatory style and near demagogic following would do the movement no good. In 1836 O'Connor founded a paper in Leeds called the *Northern Star*. By February 1838 it was selling over 10,000 copies a week and by September it had become the Chartist paper, regardless of the opposition of other leaders.

The Birmingham and London branches wished for the respectable image of responsible working men, but in the northern cities, O'Connor's emotional style attracted many supporters. Meetings became too big to be housed indoors and they moved outside to the moors behind the houses.

Above: William Cobbett (1762–1835), editor of The Political Register and author of Rural Rides – 'the freeborn Englishman incarnate'. Cobbett was a champion of sturdy, rural individualism, and many of the agricultural labourers took his vision of rural independence with them to the towns

O'Connor revelled in the crowded halls, the twilight moors, flaring torch-lights and the shouts from the crowds. He made no rational approach, but used sarcasm, abuse and comedy to make his points.

In 1839 the Charter was rejected by Parliament and O'Connor roared from the *Northern Star* against Parliament. He was prosecuted and found guilty of publishing seditious libel and was sentenced to 18 months in York jail. The Charter was submitted to Parliament again in May 1842 and similarly rejected.

On 7 May 1842, O'Connor wrote an article in the *Northern Star* that was to change his life. The Chartists must gain more political power before they could succeed, he wrote. Either the movement must ally itself with the property-owning middle class, who had the vote, or it must create voters. The idea of an alliance with the middle class he thought impracticable, so he recommended a plan for the settlement of large numbers on the land, each man occupying freehold property to the annual value of 40 shillings required to qualify for a country vote. In the following April and May, a series of letters addressed to the Producers of Wealth appeared in the *Northern Star.* They suggested that 20,000 acres could support 5,000 families with 4 acres per family in roughly 40 estates, each estate with its own school, library, hospital and community centre. The success of the scheme and the increased Chartist vote would force the government to organize more estates. Moreover life on the land was presented as the life of freedom and was seen as a way out of the degradation of the so-called 'hungry forties'.

In April 1845, he persuaded the Chartist Conference to support the idea and it was agreed to found a 'Chartist Co-operative Land Society'. This scheme appeared to be simple, but the fact that the lucky settlers were to

Above: The Charterville Estate near Minster Lovell, Oxfordshire from the Illustrated London News of 1848. The Chartist land plan attracted over 70,000 subscribers
Left: Fergus O'Connor (1796–1855), one of the Chartist leaders, editor of The Northern Star and founder of the Chartist Cooperative Land Society

be picked by lottery gave them very serious problems in getting legal status. O'Connor did not want to change his plan, but he could only get legal status if he was willing to remove the lottery. A private Act of Parliament was the only real recourse he had, and, slim though his chances were, O'Connor became convinced that only the success of their parliamentary aims could give them the necessary recognition. He decided to gamble on the scheme, but maintained the impression that they were constantly seeking legal status.

This gamble and the nature of the administration of the scheme were its ultimate downfall. But in 1846 and 1847 he was riding on an ever-expanding bubble, based on the hope of land. The *Northern Star* ran a whole series of articles on small farm management, crops and manure and whether a man could keep his family on four acres. In March 1846, O'Connor bought the first piece of land for the Society. The settlement, later to be called O'Connorville, was at Heronsgate near Rickmansworth. It cost O'Connor £1,860, but since the company had no legal status, it could not hold property, so O'Connor signed the contract and became it's owner.

By 1847 the Society had changed its name to the apparently more respectable National Co-operative Land Company and had 600 farmers throughout the country. By June, it owned 846 acres of land on four estates, and by November 1847, had spent £33,982 in buying land.

Between August 1847 and January 1848, 42,000 members were added, and receipts in these five months averaged over £5,000 a week. The fever was at its height, but the company's fragile administration could no longer cope. Increasing criticism was made in the press about the scheme and doubts were raised about O'Connor's sincerity. In August 1847 he had been elected Member of Parliament for Nottingham, and in the following February he introduced a bill into the House of Commons to legalize the company. A select committee was appointed to examine it.

Its enquiries devastated the company, demonstrating the woeful administration, half moves towards legal status, the buying of property in defiance of legal instructions and the inadequacies of the company's finance planning. Moreover the company was only able to locate 1/35th of its shareholders.

The verdict was that O'Connor's bill to legalize the company was

O'CONNORVILLE

The first ESTATE purchased by the
CHARTIST CO-OPERATIVE LAND COMPANY.

HERTFORDSHIRE.

PLAN OF THE ESTATE,

SHOWING THE POSITION OF EACH ALLOTMENT.

useless, that the company was illegal and would not match the expectations of directors or shareholders, and that the records had been most imperfectly kept. It tottered ahead for the next three years, but in 1851 a bill was passed in Parliament to wind it up. The company was dissolved, and over the next few years the estates were sold into private hands.

This was the end of O'Connor's bold experiment. The company destroyed itself by the idea of a lottery and by bad administration, but without the lottery it is very doubtful whether people would have risked the little money they had. Ill-fated though the venture was, the very commitment of so many people testifies to the strength of the myth of an agricultural utopia. Although Marx and Engels rejected the idea out of hand when O'Connor visited them in 1845, there were, nonetheless, 70,000 working people and their families who were prepared to back their myths with their money.

Left: A commemorative painting of O'Connorville near Rickmansworth
Below: Thomas Meyrick and Philip Ford and family (bottom) were amongst the original inhabitants
Below right: This handbill for the sale of the estate tells the story of what O'Connor achieved – and lost

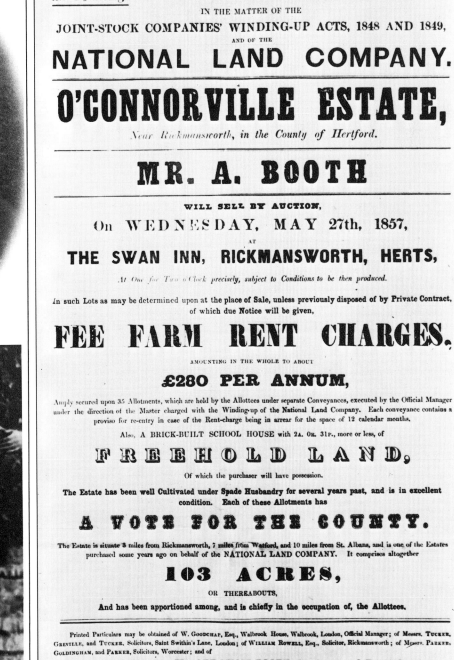

In Chancery.

IN THE MATTER OF THE

JOINT-STOCK COMPANIES' WINDING-UP ACTS, 1848 AND 1849,

AND OF THE

NATIONAL LAND COMPANY.

O'CONNORVILLE ESTATE,

Near Rickmansworth, in the County of Hertford.

MR. A. BOOTH

WILL SELL BY AUCTION,

On WEDNESDAY, MAY 27th, 1857,

AT

THE SWAN INN, RICKMANSWORTH, HERTS,

At One for Two o'Clock precisely, subject to Conditions to be then produced.

In such Lots as may be determined upon at the place of Sale, unless previously disposed of by Private Contract, of which due Notice will be given,

FEE FARM RENT CHARGES,

AMOUNTING IN THE WHOLE TO ABOUT

£280 PER ANNUM,

Amply secured upon 35 Allotments, which are held by the Allottees under separate Conveyances, executed by the Official Manager under the direction of the Master charged with the Winding-up of the National Land Company. Each conveyance contains a proviso for re-entry in case of the Rent-charge being in arrear for the space of 12 calendar months,

Also, A BRICK-BUILT SCHOOL HOUSE with 2a. 0r. 31r., more or less, of

FREEHOLD LAND,

Of which the purchaser will have possession.

The Estate has been well Cultivated under Spade Husbandry for several years past, and is in excellent condition. Each of these Allotments has

A VOTE FOR THE COUNTY.

The Estate is situate 3 miles from Rickmansworth, 7 miles from Watford, and 10 miles from St. Albans, and is one of the Estates purchased some years ago on behalf of the NATIONAL LAND COMPANY. It comprises altogether

103 ACRES,

OR THEREABOUTS,

And has been apportioned among, and is chiefly in the occupation of, the Allottees.

Printed Particulars may be obtained of W. GOODCHAP, Esq., Walbrook House, Walbrook, London, Official Manager; of Messrs. TUCKER, GREVILLE, and TUCKER, Solicitors, Saint Swithin's Lane, London; of WILLIAM ROWELL, Esq., Solicitor, Rickmansworth; of Messrs. PARKER, GOLDINGHAM, and PARKER, Solicitors, Worcester; and of

Mr. ABRAHAM BOOTH, Auctioneer and Estate Agent,

1, CARLTON HILL VILLAS, CAMDEN ROAD, LONDON.

THE CRISIS,

OR THE CHANGE FROM ERROR AND MISERY, TO TRUTH AND HAPPINESS.

1832.

IF WE CANNOT YET

LET US ENDEAVOUR

RECONCILE ALL OPINIONS,

TO UNITE ALL HEARTS.

IT IS OF ALL TRUTHS THE MOST IMPORTANT, THAT THE CHARACTER OF MAN IS FORMED FOR—NOT BY HIMSELF.

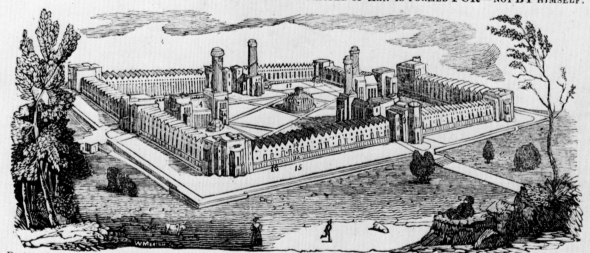

Design of a Community of 2,000 Persons, founded upon a principle, commended by Plato, Lord Bacon, Sir T. More, & R. Owen.

EDITED BY

ROBERT OWEN AND ROBERT DALE OWEN.

London:

PRINTED AND PUBLISHED BY J. EAMONSON, 15, CHICHESTER PLACE, GRAY'S INN ROAD.

STRANGE, PATERNOSTER ROW. PURKISS, OLD COMPTON STREET, AND MAY BE HAD OF ALL BOOKSELLERS.

Harmony: Utopia in the New World

Left: Robert Owen's journal The Crisis, featuring Steadman Whitwell's architectural plan for the ideal community: 'the community of 2,000 persons founded upon the principles of Plato, Lord Bacon, Sir T. More and R. Owen'

While the French Revolution demonstrated that radical political change was possible, it took the industrial revolution to bring the economic and social changes that radically altered the daily lives of millions. During the early years of the nineteenth century, theorists such as Robert Owen, Charles Fourier and Henri de Saint-Simon developed their plans to bring order and harmony into the chaos and competition that surrounded them. At the time they were known as 'socialists', simply because they had a theory of society, but they later became known as the 'Utopian socialists' and the name has stuck. However, their influence was not confined to ideas and plans and many utopian experiments grew out of their theories.

Robert Owen and Owenism

In 1799, Robert Owen, 28 years old and partner in a Manchester spinning business, travelled north to Scotland to meet David Dale, lay preacher, philanthropist, and owner of one of the largest spinning mills in Britain. Owen began the new century in style: in September 1799 he married the daughter of David Dale, and on 1 January 1800 he set up partnership with her father to run the mills at New Lanark in Scotland.

Under Owen's leadership, New Lanark became the most famous industrial community of the early nineteenth century, while remaining one of the most profitable. Lanark was not, nor was it ever intended to be, utopia, but it was the culmination of Owen's industrial experiment and it convinced him that, given the opportunity, utopia was possible. This was a belief that never left him, even in the light of his later failures in North America.

Owen's career spanned the first stage of the industrial revolution in

Britain. When he was born, Britain was still a rural country, its population was dispersed, transport was by horse or water, and its produce was mainly agricultural. He died in 1858, seven years after the Great Exhibition had been mounted to celebrate the industrial and imperial success of Great Britain. The population had been forced into towns and cities, the major railway lines were almost complete, coal provided the bulk of the nation's power, and industry had become such an abundant source of wealth that the country had long ago ceased to be self-sufficient in food production.

Owen had made his fortune in the industry that had led the industrial revolution—cotton—and in the pioneering town—Manchester. The move to Lanark gave him the opportunity to put ideas he had been developing in Manchester into practice. He began by raising the minimum working age to ten and reducing the hours of actual work. Private retail stores were closed down and replaced by a single community store which sold good-quality food and goods 25 per cent cheaper than the previous price for poor quality. He even undercut the cheap spirits with good whisky.

Each week a deduction was made from wages to cover sick pay and retirement, and during a slump in the cotton trade, he paid wages in full for three months although production had stopped. Although wages were slightly lower than elsewhere, social provisions were incomparably greater, and the combination of philanthropy and discipline won the confidence of the workforce and produced results. Owen could write, echoing the Potteries industrialist Josiah Wedgwood before him, that

Below: The enlightened Mr Owen, benevolent industrialist and materialist thinker, believed that 'the character of man is made for him and not by him.' His theories led him to set up pioneering communities as the basis for a 'new moral world'

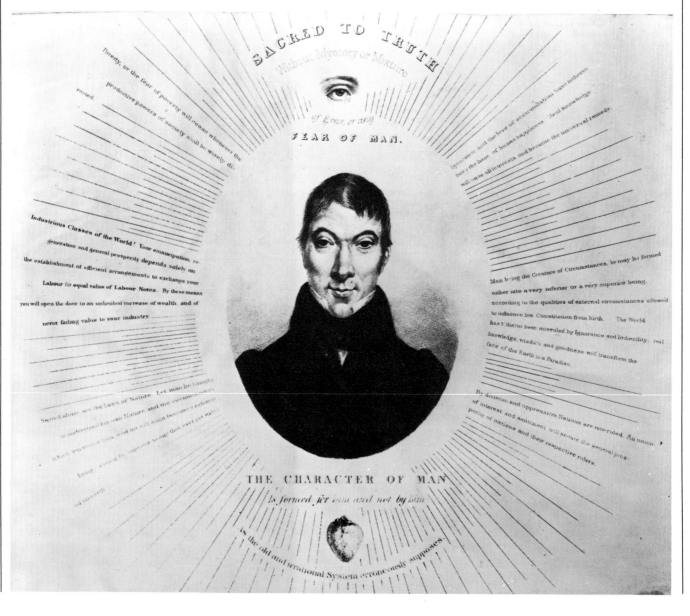

'an idle dirty, dissolute and drunken population was transformed by the application of proper means into one of order, neatness and regularity'.

The widespread misery and awful living conditions of the new industrial working class were already a scandal when Owen took over New Lanark. He had set out to prove that they were not the inevitable result of industrialization or of profit, and in this attitude there is little to separate him from other philanthropic industrialists. But Owen went further: his programme at Lanark did not stem merely from philanthropy, business efficiency or a feeling of duty towards his workers, but from his belief that the 'character of man is made FOR him and not BY him'. Thus he thought that, by changing the conditions of people's lives, it should be possible to change their characters. The final aim of character formation, he believed, should be happiness, for the production of happiness 'will be the only religion of man'.

His early success in Manchester and Lanark convinced him of the truth of his philosophy, and of the need to begin character formation as early as possible in a person's life. The first infant school in Britain was opened at New Lanark, and children attended from the time they could walk. Their characters were to be formed in the 'natural' pursuit of happiness, through games, dances, attractive colourful visual aids, 'familiar conversations', and 'military exercises' (calisthenics), but with the minimum of bookish learning. Through a consistent, kind and non-violent regime, with no 'artificial' rewards or punishments, a child was to develop a sense of community and an understanding of 'the necessary consequences, immediate and remote, which result from any action'. The schools put Owen in the forefront of educational reform, and New Lanark became famous. Visitors, including the Tsar of Russia, came from far and wide to see the dancing children. Owen himself became a celebrity, and his opinions were listened to with respect.

In 1815, at the end of the Napoleonic War, the outbreak of peace brought a slump in the market, cuts in wages and production, and an increase in poverty and unemployment. In response Owen proposed the setting up of self-sufficient agricultural colonies. These 'Villages of Co-operation' for 300 to 2000 poor people engaged in 'spade agriculture' were the beginning of his utopian communities. Radicals opposed the scheme (Cobbett called them 'parallelograms of Paupers'), but the establishment, including the Archbishop of Canterbury, the Duke of York, the Home Secretary and the Prime Minister, gave cautious approval.

Owen presented his proposals to parliament, but met with little success so he published his report and began an unprecedented publicity cam-

Above: At the New Lanark school for the children of Owen's mill-hands, characters were to be formed in the 'natural' pursuit of happiness, through games, dances, attractive, colourful visual aids and calisthenics

Top: The New Lanark Mill as the artist saw it in the early nineteenth century
Above: New Lanark today. After many years of neglect a trust has been set up to preserve it. It was the first step on a utopian trail which later took Owen to America

paign. Soon he declared that the proposed communities would be so pleasant that he himself would like to retire to one, and a little later he claimed that they could transform society and inaugurate the 'New Moral World'. In the meantime, at a meeting in the City of London Tavern in August 1817, he had publicly attacked the 'gross errors of every religion that has hitherto been taught to man'. This tactless display of his anti-clericalism put paid to any hope of public or state backing for good.

In 1824, however, Owen was presented with the opportunity to put the whole of his theory into practice on a grand scale. He was approached by Richard Flower, an Englishman who had been commissioned by the Rappite community of Harmony, Indiana, to dispose of their property. The followers of George Rapp formed a celibate community based on the Pentecostal church. Rapp had arrived in America from Germany in 1803 and had founded a successful community in Pennsylvania before moving to Indiana in 1814, where, within ten years they built up the community of Harmony. But the Rappites' relationship with the neighbouring farmers was poor and they were troubled by malaria, so they decided to move on and wished to sell as soon as possible.

Owen struck a hard bargain, and for 150,000 dollars bought economically proven assets sufficient for a thousand persons:

> 30,000 acres of land with 3,000 under cultivation by the company, 19 detached farms, 600 acres of improved land occupied by tenants; some fine orchards; 18 acres of full-bearing vines; and the village . . . a regularly laid out town, with streets running at right angles to each other and a public square, around which were high edifices, built by the Rappites for churches, schools, and other public purposes.

On 27 April 1825, George Rapp's Harmony became Robert Owen's New Harmony and America's first secular utopian experiment began. Almost immediately its founder returned to England leaving an interim constitution intended to operate for three years.

During the ensuing 'honeymoon' period, a school and a band were formed, but the community produced very little. Owen returned the following year, cut short the three-year transitional phase, and inaugurated the 'New Harmony Community of Equals'. Ironically this led to the first split, and William Maclure and his followers set up Macluria on another part of

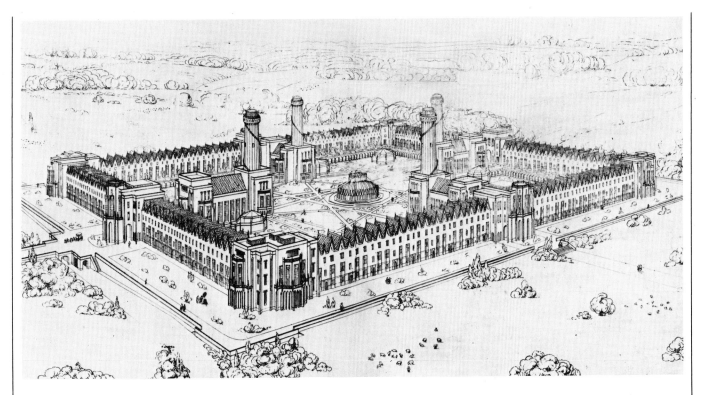

the estate. However, the two communities were on friendly terms, and for a while, under Owen's direction, things seemed to be going according to plan. However, in April 1826 disputes arose about the ultimate ownership of the property and the form of government. Neither was ever resolved, and in May a third group was formed called Feiba Peven.

Despite these setbacks, Owen's sense of occasion did not desert him, and on 4 July 1826, the fiftieth anniversary of the American Declaration of Independence, he issued his *Declaration of Mental Independence*. This declared liberation from the 'monstrous evils' of 'Private or Individual Property, Absurd or Irrational systems of Religion and Marriage founded on Individual Property' and claimed that New Harmony was the beginning of the millennium.

Further disputes led to Owen being accepted as sole director, on top of his role as spiritual leader and in confirmation of his key position. However, all the old problems remained and the experiment was falling apart. Owen had lost a great deal of money, and tried to retrieve it by selling off parts of the estate and town. Eventually he left in June 1827 leaving the land in the hands of his children and William Maclure.

The experience at New Harmony influenced religious and secular communities for half a century. If people learn from mistakes, or from 'the necessary consequences of their actions' as Owen would put it, then it should have been the most excellent lesson, for almost every mistake was made. First and foremost, they moved to a ready-made township, so that members had none of the satisfaction of building the place up for themselves. This in itself drew sarcastic comment from the religious communities. John Humphrey Noyes, founder of the long-lived Oneida Community, wrote that the Rappites spent their 'ten best years building a town not for themselves, but for a theatre of the great infidel experiment'.

The ready-built 'theatre' naturally attracted people avoiding the necessary discipline and hard work of a real frontier situation, and the problem was aggravated by the 'open door' policy of uncontrolled entry. Furthermore, despite all his talk of equality and co-operation in the millennium, Owen was no democrat during the transition period and he consistently held power of veto on all decisions. For all this, the experience was not entirely negative, and New Harmony left its mark, either as an inspiration or as a catalogue of errors. Indeed Harmony itself remained a place of experiment for many years particularly in its schools and in the curious 'Time Shop' of Joseph Warren.

Top: The plan for purpose-built premises to accommodate an Owenite community
Above: Harmony, Indiana as Robert Owen bought it from George Rapp in 1825. For 150,000 dollars Owen bought economically proven assets sufficient for a thousand persons and America's first secular utopian experiment began

Joseph Warren was a remarkable man of many and varied parts. He had been at New Harmony with Owen, and it is likely that he devised the labour note system that Owen tried to start in England during his involvement with the Trade Union Movement. His response to Owen's emphasis on communalism was to develop a doctrine of Individual Sovereignty. 'Peace, harmony, ease, security and happiness', he said, 'will be found only in Individuality'. Thus every individual, male or female, should do exactly as they liked, with the one condition that the individual should carry the entire cost of this freedom, for they had 'no right to tax the community for the consequences of their deeds'.

In 1842 he returned to New Harmony from England and started a Time Shop. Goods were paid for with ordinary money for the material or wholesale costs, but with vouchers for the time taken in preparing and actually selling the article. This 'labour content' of the goods was paid in Time Notes which were in widespread circulation. Everyone made their own notes according to the value they put on their own labour, but if they over-valued it, then people would not be prepared to take the 'inflated' notes so their value automatically dropped.

The system was a direct implementation of a primitive labour theory of value, and in a frontier society, where people knew each other well, it worked efficiently. More money was effectively put into circulation, and it became possible for people to trade their labour in an equal relationship. But when Owen tried a modified version in London, Brighton and Birmingham, in a much more complex and varied economic situation, his labour exchanges became dumping grounds for unsaleable goods and the value of his labour notes dropped.

Warren and his followers later moved to Cincinnatti where they took over the site of a failed community and founded a village which they called Utopia. Later still they went to Long Island and founded 'Modern Times', a community which became notorious in respectable society as a den of 'free love' and 'anarchism', but which seems to have worked successfully. In contrast to Owen's proselytizing, principles of philosophy, moralizing, and reputedly boring and interminable lectures, Warren based Utopia on the most basic individualism, and in consequence, 'not one meeting for legislation has taken place. No organization, no delegated power, no constitutions, no laws or bye-laws, rules or regulations, but

Below: The labour note introduced by Owen for trade in the National Equitable Labour Exchanges which were set up in London, Brighton and Birmingham. Within a few months the stores were stocked with unwanted goods and the labour notes were worthless

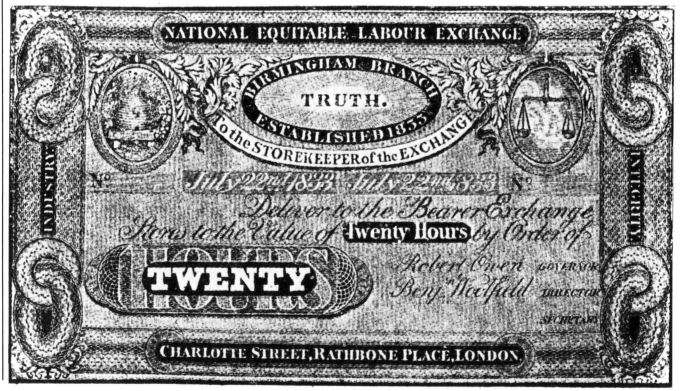

NEW HARMONY — All Owin'— No payin

such as each individual makes for himself and his own business: no officers, no priests nor prophets have been resorted to; nothing of this kind has been in demand.'

Owen had an effect not only in America, but also in Britain, and communities were set up there too. Owen himself was involved in those at Orbiston, Rahaline and Queenwood, the last of which ran from 1839 to 1845 and was the final Owenite community in Britain.

Curiously, his schemes were longer lived outside the main Owenite movement. John Minter Morgan was an early follower of Owen, and had popularized his ideas in two utopian novels, *The Revolt of the Bees* and *Hampden in the Nineteenth Century.* When he left the Owenite movement to return to the Church of England, he took with him the scheme for 'self-supporting colonies for the poor'. In the 1840s, revamped as *A Christian Commonwealth,* it was still being considered seriously within the church, and a petition was presented to Parliament in 1845.

Although Morgan, like Owen, cites Plato, More and Bacon, his ambitions are far more modest than those of Owen, and he makes it abundantly clear that his scheme 'involves no change in the existing order of society, being intended solely for the unemployed and destitute poor, who will maintain their present relative position'. Even if success led to a proliferation of communities there was still no threat, for 'all the valuable Institutions of Society' would be 'materially strengthened and extended, since a church and schools are required for every 300 families located upon the principle proposed'. *A Christian Commonwealth* expressed unambiguously the thinking that radicals such as Cobbett had feared was behind the idea when it was first proposed by Owen.

Curiously, for a man who had made his fortune in the cotton industry, Owen's 'New Moral World' was not dependent on the increased wealth brought about by industry and technology. In this he reflects the widespread feeling that industrial capitalism, with its social upheaval and inhuman conditions, was unnatural and could not last—hence the expectation of the millennium and the readiness to go into the wilderness to construct a portion of heaven or a microcosm of the new age.

Such groups and communities were legion: Rappites, Essenes, Shakers, Ephratans, Moravians, Perfectionists, Jansenites and more, all strove for a perfect world at Harmony, Bishops Hill, Brook Farm, Yellow Springs, Bohemia Manor, and a thousand other places. A single example will serve to illustrate the bizarre diversity of custom and belief; the Shakers believed that the Second Coming had already occurred in the person of their leader Ann Lee, known as 'Ann the Word'. Thus they believed that each of their villages was literally a small part of the Garden of Eden.

Ann Lee and her first followers were mill-hands and mechanics from Manchester who emigrated to Albany, New York, in 1774. By the middle of the nineteenth century they had 6000 members in 18 villages, despite the fact that the communities were completely celibate and had to rely on outside recruitment in order to survive. The punishment for sexual contact was expulsion. Life revolved around the religious meeting with ecstatic whirling dances that culminated in complete shaking abandon. Although they kept their needs and material possessions to a minimum, their lives were by no means spartan. Craft skill was welcomed and valued, and their unadorned traditional houses and furniture have an elegance rarely found in communist communities. Their theology incorporated both male and female as equals and so it was natural that they should practise complete egalitarianism of the sexes. Indeed it was a Shaker woman, Sister Tabitha Babbitt, who invented the powered circular saw in 1810.

Charles Fourier

The enthusiasm for the Owenite utopia in America had virtually subsided by 1830, and was followed by ten years of intense religious revivalism. But the early 1840s saw a fresh outbreak of secular utopianism, inspired by the theories of the Frenchman Charles Fourier.

Fourier was not content to educate people to happiness as Owen was, or to inspire co-operation through a rational religion, as other utopians such as his wealthy compatriot Saint-Simon recommended. He thought that both these practices were just as much distortions of people's 'natural' and instinctive selves as were the practices of the existing society. Rather the new society should be based on a science of human relationships, and he believed that he had discovered that science in his 'theory of passional attraction'.

A 'passional attraction', he wrote, 'is the drive that is given to us by nature prior to any reflection, and it persists despite the opposition of reason, duty, or prejudice.' Nature intended that the passions should be gratified, and that if thwarted, these natural passions inevitably led to chaos. Perfect harmony, he thought, lay in complete gratification. As a

Above: An illustration from Minter Morgan's A Christian Commonwealth, which accommodated the Established Church within a scheme similar to Owen's early projects
Above right: The ecstatic dance begins at a Shaker religious gathering in New York City in 1873
Right: The plan of the Harvard Shaker Community, 1836. Shaker theology regarded males and females as equals. Women provided leadership and played a prominent role in their communities

psychological theory, this leads to completely opposite conclusions to Freud, who thought that, although people may *strive* for complete, immediate and never-ending gratification of their passions, in practice they had to be redirected and repressed if people were to live in society.

Fourier developed his theory in minute detail over a period of nearly 40 years. He analysed personality into different combinations and strengths of passions, in ascending and descending 'series'. He invented ideal working and social groups in which the passions would be in equilibrium, for different passions were shown to have their main influence at different stages in people's lives. A system of geometry, in which each passion had a characteristic shape, described the 'harmonic' inter-relationship of people and passions; and diagrams charts, plans, schedules and timetables gave a precise description of daily life in the ideal community, down to the sexual life of its citizens.

Fourier's father had been a cloth merchant in Besançon, and he intended that his son should follow him in the trade. Fourier hated the life and tried to escape from 'the workshops of deceit', but he was eventually induced to remain in his third apprenticeship—his inheritance was conditional on his entering the trade. Ironically he lost most of that in Lyon during the French Revolution and he was forced to take employment in the clothing business in order to survive.

For the rest of his life he worked as a clerk, and lived on his own in boarding houses with his cats and 'harmonic' flower arrangements. Each day followed a strict routine, with all his energy and money devoted to his writing. Most of his books were published at his own expense and distributed free to potential backers. For many years after the publication of the *New Industrial and Social World,* Fourier returned to his lodgings each day at midday to await the benefactor who would put his ideas into practice. On one occasion the French Minister of Public Works showed an interest, but the July Revolution of 1830 intervened, the government fell, and the promised meeting never occurred.

Fourier's ideal community, The Phalanx, was to be inhabited by 1620 people divided into 16 tribes and 32 choirs. More or less might be per-

Below: Charles Fourier (1772–1837). His utopian vision was based on the belief that people's natural 'passions' should be gratified Bottom: An illustration from V. Considèrant's book shows how the ideal Fourierist Phalanstère or village would look

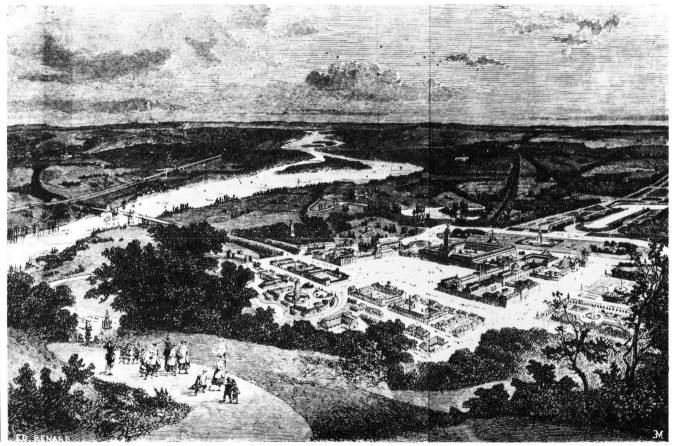

mitted, but care must be taken to ensure an adequate variety of passions. No existing buildings would be suitable, not even the vast palaces at Versailles, so a new social palace, or phalanstery, was to be constructed. At its centre would be dining rooms, the exchange, meeting rooms, library, studies, a temple, a tower, a telegraph, coops for carrier pigeons, ceremonial chimes, an observatory and a winter courtyard adorned by 'resinous' plants.

Various wings would contain all workshops and education, ballrooms, residences and a place for visitors, 'who should not be allowed to encumber the centre of the palace and to disturb the domestic relations of the Phalanx'. Indeed the trial Phalanx had to be protected from visitors. The whole complex was to be linked by covered street galleries. 'In harmony one can pass through the workshops, stables, shops, ballrooms, banquet and assembly halls etc in January without knowing whether it is windy, hot or cold.'

People were to work at a wide variety of jobs, and change jobs very frequently, several times in each day. Each person would do a minimum amount of work and receive a basic wage. Above that, people's wages could be as varied as they wished to make them by the amount and kind of work they decided to do, though there should be no moral or social pressure exerted to make people work. By making work attractive, Fourier hoped to liberate people from the work ethic as well as from the drudgery of work. The more difficult, uncomfortable or unrewarding the work, the higher was the wage paid for it.

Fourier had little faith in the type of family in which he had been brought up. In the dreams conjured in his hotel room, he replaces the family with a system of free love, with equality between the sexes, and with the Phalanx as a whole taking on the responsibilities for welfare and children. He envisaged a situation where marriage and the conventional sexual customs of society were not just abolished but forgotten, so that their absence would inspire a 'host of amorous innovations which we cannot yet imagine'. 'Voluptuousness', he wrote, 'is the sole arm which God can employ to master us and lead us to carry out his designs: he rules the universe by attraction and not by force.'

Most of Fourier's writings on sexual relationships were suppressed by his immediate followers as were his crazier historical notions. Victor Considérant and his fellow disciples felt that such ideas might not be beneficial to the movement, but they retained the basic theory of the passions, the plans for communities, the emphasis on everyday life, attractive work, and sexual equality and liberation. Their aims were to be achieved by small groups taking direct control over their immediate social relationships. Their first community, at Condé-sur-Vesgre near Rambouillet, was shortlived. It was small, and infuriated Fourier as a travesty of his ideas, so he was neither sorry nor surprised to see it collapse.

Later in the century, the industrialist Godin, who made cast-iron kitchenware, set up his factory at Guise as a modified version of the Fourierist Phalanx. Godin himself lived out his life in this *Familistère*—a communal residential building in which each family had a separate flat linked around a glass-covered courtyard with street galleries on all levels. The buildings are still in use today, although its inhabitants are no longer exclusively employed in Godin's Factory.

After Fourier's death in 1837, many of his followers, led by Considérant, went to America, where the ideas were popularized by the journalist Albert Brisbane. America came out in a rash of shortlived communities, the most successful being the North American Phalanx in New Jersey and the Wisconsin Phalanx. The former was crippled by fire in 1854 after 12 years and the property sold off. The Wisconsin Phalanx thrived, became very rich, but in December 1849, after only five years, the community voted to sell up. They split the proceeds, and became wealthy individuals instead of a wealthy community.

Fourier had conceived his theory around 1800 and for most of his life his work was treated with derision. The Fourierist movement did not develop until 30 years later and might have remained much smaller had it not been for a split amongst the followers of Count Henri de Saint-Simon.

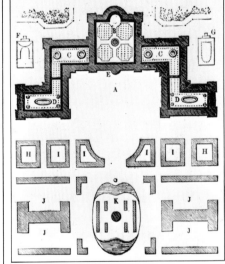

Above: All the various plans produced by Fourier and his followers used the Palace of Versailles as a model, with the implication that all might live in luxury

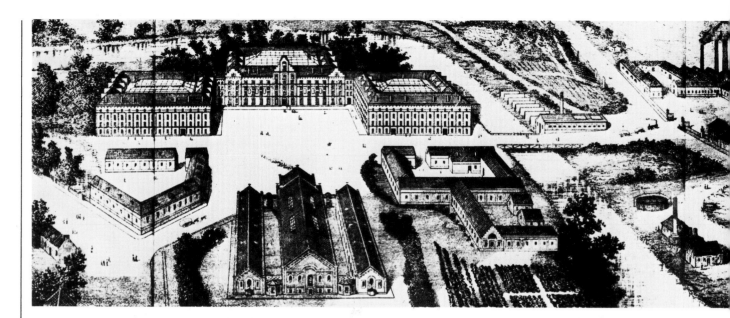

Saint-Simon

Saint-Simon had been born into one of France's wealthiest families in 1760. He was 11 years older than Owen and Fourier, and so saw the American revolution as well as the French. Although he lost his inheritance through a family dispute between his father and uncle, he never lost his aristocratic sense of importance and destiny. For many years his valet would wake him with the words, 'Arise, Monsieur le Comte, you have great deeds to perform.'

At 17, he went to America to see the revolution at first hand. He returned dedicated to the study 'of the movements of the human mind that I might labour for the perfection of civilization'. Unlike Fourier, he believed that civilization was a good thing. As a true follower of the philosophers of the Enlightenment and of Francis Bacon, he saw scientific progress as the path to society's perfection. Saint-Simon's proposals for society were neither democratic nor egalitarian, but he would remove the lower level of poverty and the top level of aristocratic parasites.

The aim of society and religion should be the 'raising of the condition of the poor to an acceptable level', rather than removing the distinction between rich and poor. People could become as rich as they would, but by their own talents and efforts. Thus he opposed all inherited wealth or unearned income, and all land, capital and the means of production were to be owned by the state. Political control would rest with three groups, organized in three chambers—Invention, Examination and Executive. In the first two chambers were to be scientists, engineers and inventors—the élite of talent and expertise—while the third group was to be made up of Entrepreneurs, Bankers and Industrialists. This executive held power, but was controlled by the intellectuals and men and women of genius.

The result should be an ideal meritocracy in which people would benefit from the full development of their talents and in which the play of these talents would be fully rewarded. 'All my life is comprised of this thought; to guarantee to all men the freest development of their faculties.' Towards the end of his life Saint-Simon developed his new Christianity which would be the social glue that would hold the system together. It would promote brotherhood and mutual love, and so take the aggressive edge from the competitiveness implicit in an individualist meritocracy.

Etienne Cabet

The system of Saint-Simon rests on the 'natural inequality of people', and the belief that these inequalities should flourish. In complete contrast were those political activists, following early French communists like Morelly, who believed in complete and absolute equality.

Above: The Familistère at Guise, a communal residential building built by the industrialist André Godin (1817–1888). Godin was an ardent follower of Fourier and lived there among his workers·
Left: The Count Henri de Saint-Simon (1760–1825). He proposed a utopia where government would be directed and checked by the new industrial experts
Right: The Saint-Simonian emancipated female. Her pantaloons were to ensure greater freedom of movement. Saint-Simon once wrote to his celebrated contemporary Madame De Staël, suggesting that between them they could beget a genius!

One such activist was Etienne Cabet, who was a leading member of the Carbonari, a conspiratorial revolutionary group dedicated like Babeuf's Conspiracy of Equals to total equality. As a result of his activities in the revolution of 1830, and later in Corsica, he was sentenced to imprisonment, but succeeded in escaping to London. There he met Robert Owen, read Thomas More's *Utopia* and became a convinced utopian.

From 1834 to 1839 he toiled away in the British Museum to produce the *Voyage to Icaria,* the bible of Icarian Communism. He said:

> I wrote the *Voyage to Icaria* to place before the world the example of a great nation having a community of goods. At the same time I perceived that this community could not be established after Babeuf's plan, by conspiracy and violence, but by means of discussion, by propagandism, by persuasion, and the force of public opinion.

Voyage to Icaria was an immediate success and inspired an Icarian movement. It describes a visit to Icaria, a utopian island, made by Cabet in the company of an English aristocrat, Lord Carisdale, who is there to provide romantic interest, ask unintelligent questions, and to show that even the aristocracy can be converted. The state, founded in 1782 by the liberator Icar, comprises 100 provinces divided into six communes, each with a town, eight villages and various farms. In the centre of the country stands the capital—affluent, cultured, circular and symmetrical, with 100 straight wide streets.

Icaria is a country of order and physical abundance, 'covered with the green harvest', with vines, 'flowery arbours', groves, plantations and picturesque villages. Similarly abundant is the virtue of its population with no idlers, drunkards, thieves or adulterers. All Icarians are equal; they use the same furniture, keep to the same precise timetable, wear the same clothes, live in identical houses, receive the same education and are all equally happy and satisfied. Everything is made possible by direct and representative democracy.

Each commune elects delegates to a national assembly and votes directly for a sixteen-person executive whose members head the key committees of agriculture, industry, furniture, food, clothing and education. They are re-elected every six months. At commune level all the inhabitants are part of a commune assembly which must discuss and agree all laws and arrangements. Both national and communal assemblies have their committees which discuss and make recommendations. Every detail of daily life is decided by this hierarchy of committees, and, because everyone decides, everyone is happy with the decisions. Take for instance the daily timetable:

> Have you noticed the regular movement of our population? At five o'clock, everyone gets up; as six approaches, all our public vehicles and the streets are full of men going to their factories; at nine, the women and children appear; from nine to one, the population is in the factories or the schools; at one-thirty, the whole mass of workers leave the factories to join their families and neighbours in the people's restaurants; from two to three, everyone eats; from three to nine, the entire population goes out into the gardens, streets, terraces, promenades, popular assemblies, lecture halls, theatres and other public places; at ten, everyone goes to bed; and during the night, from ten to five o'clock, the streets are deserted. . . . A curfew imposed by a tyrant would be an intolerable vexation; but adopted by an entire people in the interests of its health and of good order in work, it is the most reasonable and useful of our laws.

Working hours have been kept to a minimum, and mass production has brought the whole population to a state of plenty, every household having the identical accoutrements of wealth:

> Last year, for example, when a new piece of furniture was added to the furniture which we then had in each household, a hundred thousand workers were needed to produce it; accordingly we took the hundred thousand workers from the mass of the labouring masses and increased the daily period of general work by five minutes.

Everyone works in field or factory, which operate under a form of worker's control, although women work shorter hours in the factory to compensate for the hours spent at housework. Only women who run households are fully exempt from factory work. Men begin work at 18 and women at 17 with exemption at 60 and 50 respectively, although few take up the exemption as work has been made easy by machines.

Icaria is an idealized industrial system, taking mass production to a logical conclusion, with uniformity of product, consumption, social life, timetable, and presumably of the workers themselves. The only diversity comes from a sexual division of labour in which some jobs are thought suitable for women and others for men. Marriages are made after consultation with parents, and would-be partners may spend as much time as they like together before marriage, as long as the parents are there with them. At the sumptuous dances only married couples are allowed to dance together, otherwise men dance with men and women with women.

The whole social machine and its vast network of committees runs without any bureaucratic establishment, and each executive member returns to his or her trade between committee meetings. Each community has its own newspaper, which only prints facts and whose editor is elected. Only good books are printed and that too is decided by committee. Priests, if people want them, are elected for terms of six months, though the usual religion is a silent worship similar to that of de Foigney. Clothing is decided by committee and everyone has a full wardrobe with different outfits for different occasions and different times of the day. There is even a committee of Christians whose job it is to judge the dead.

Through his obsession with equality, Cabet creates an imaginary society in which individuality has completely disappeared. Icaria was not the product of democratic committees, but of a literary dictator sitting alone in a library in a country whose language he did not understand. It is easily open to parody and provides the kind of characterization that gave communism a bad name.

By 1847 Cabet had decided to put his teachings into practice. Land was bought at Red River in Texas and 69 prospective Icarians set out in February 1848. They believed they had bought a 1,000,000 acres, but when they arrived, found only 100,000 acres, divided into small lots, with the stipulation that each lot should have a farmhouse on it within a year. On top of this the 69 pioneers were struck down by yellow fever and when Cabet arrived with another group in 1848 the remnants of the

Below: A view of the Icarian community at Nauvoo on the Mississippi. With funds from France, Cabet bought the town from the Mormons and the community began well with fifteen thousand inhabitants, until Cabet himself was expelled in 1855

group had returned to St Louis. Undeterred, and with plenty of funds being sent over from France, Cabet bought the town of Nauvoo from the Mormons, just as Owen had bought Harmony from the Rappites.

Although the community was made up mainly of French tradesmen, and thus was short on farming skills, it began well. Fifteen hundred Icarians moved in, the industries worked smoothly, a progressive school was started and an orchestra, a band and a theatre group were set up. Such was their progress that in 1850 Cabet gave up his dictatorship, which he had taken on as the personification of Icar, and he was elected director with similar powers but subject to re-election.

Gradually however, he introduced more stringent measures, banning alcohol and tobacco, and later tried to introduce a special diet and a strict puritanical sexual morality. Dissension broke out, and in 1855 a new director was elected followed by even greater disputes, conducted with street fighting, a general strike and a division into two opposing factions. The new director stopped all food supplies and the strike was broken. At a general assembly, Cabet was expelled from the community, and left for St Louis with 180 followers. He died a week later.

After two years working in St Louis, the Cabet group had saved up enough money to buy new land at Cheltenham, about 20 miles outside the city. There they began again and survived until the 1860s. The Nauvoo group moved to Corning in Iowa where they struggled on for a while until the civil war brought, along with the soldiers, a market for their produce. Nonetheless its numbers declined until the fall of the Paris Commune in 1871, after which it received an influx of young refugees who brought with them Marxist and anarchist philosophies and an emphasis on urban values of industrial production. Conflict was inevitable, and in 1879 the younger group split off and moved to California where they set up Icaria Speranza near San Francisco. Both groups flourished economically and sold out at a profit, Icaria Speranza in 1886 and Corning in 1898.

The Oneida Community, Bible Communism and Complex Marriage

A long-established laboratory for community experiment, America's communities were mainly inspired by religious movements, but for two brief periods, from 1824 to 1830 and from 1840 to 1845, the majority of the community foundations were Owenite or Fourierist, and secular. In comparison with the religious communities, they were notably unsuccessful, although they did have their effects on the religious communities themselves. The Oneida Community was one of the groups that tried to bridge the gap and become both a religious and a communist community.

Their religion taught that god was both male and female, and that the Second Coming had already occurred in AD 70; therefore people could become perfect simply by accepting Christ into their souls. The community grew up around John Humphrey Noyes in Putney, Vermont, simply as a religious sect, but when its members began to live together as a communist group on Fourierist lines the local community drove them out, and in 1848 they bought a forty-acre farm near Oneida in New York State.

Unlike many communities they were able to build up a broad economic base thanks to about 100,000 dollars in capital provided by the early members. They manufactured chains, silk thread, woollen goods, suitcases and the best-selling Newhouse animal trap. They operated a canning plant, blacksmith's shop, saw mill, and flour mill, as well as farming their land. All this brought prosperity, and the community was able to buy more land and provide the comforts that so many of the other communities had only promised.

A large neo-gothic mansion house was built, with landscaped gardens, a theatre, a progressive school, a library and a sauna bath. Work was varied, as Fourier would have intended, and flexible in its organization, with people moving from job to job. If necessary, the whole community would work together on some large order. By the mid-1870s it numbered around 250 adults and also employed a similar number of people in its various ventures. In most areas of their social life, its members followed

Above: From the time of its resettlement America has been a laboratory for communal experiments, mainly inspired by religious movements. These are typical buildings of one community in Ephrate, Pennsylvania

the radical ideas of their day. They wore simple clothes with women in short hair and trousers; they were mainly vegetarian, and used no tobacco or alcohol; children were brought up in nurseries with both male and female nurses; they regulated their relations with group criticism and self-criticism. Faith healing was practised, though they also used conventional medicine. All decisions were made at meetings of the whole community, after research and recommendation by a committee, but if a decision was in dispute then it was merely put off until everyone agreed.

Oneida had many features of the Fourierist utopia, but was most famous for its efforts to break down monogamous marriage, which Noyes saw as a religious as well as a social tyranny quite inappropriate to people seeking a perfection in which they should love everyone equally. They introduced a system of complex marriage in which the forming of exclusive couples was discouraged, and the necessity for pleasure in sexual relationships was emphasized, particularly for women.

By the practice of birth control and yoga they separated their pleasurable relationships from reproduction and were able to introduce 'stirpiculture', a eugenic experiment in which all members of the community agreed to breed only on the instructions of a special committee. Fifty-eight stirpicult children were born at Oneida between 1869 and 1879, but in that year the experiment was abandoned and Noyes himself retired to Canada. Within two years it had become a joint stock company with private ownership, but in 1899 one of Noyes's stirpicult children, Pierpoint Burt Noyes, gained effective control and turned it into an industrial co-operative community that still survives today.

From that time on, communities continued to be set up in America, and new ventures still begin today. However, the phase directly influenced by the utopian socialist theorists of Europe was over by 1900. By then home-grown theorists like Henry George were supplying the inspiration. In Europe itself, the utopian socialists had inspired fewer communities, but they had become the centre of a political debate with 'scientific socialists' still vigorously continued today and which has tended to inhibit rather than foster utopian experiment.

Right: Schoolchildren from the Middle Amana Community in Iowa circa 1890. The original members of the Amana society came from Germany in the early nineteenth century, moving west to Iowa around 1850. The society remained a religious commune until 1932
Below: The beginnings of a community, with timber houses and cabins in newly cleared forest at Atwell's Mill. It reminds us that not all communities moved into readymade towns, as did Owen

The Ideal
Without the State

When Karl Marx and Friedrich Engels, in *The Communist Manifesto* of 1848, described Saint-Simon, Fourier and Owen as utopian socialists they added yet another dimension to the term 'utopian', and gave a great boost to its career as a term of abuse. They used it to distinguish other forms of communist theory and practice from their own. In the communist view, utopians tried to think themselves out of their own epoch, by a mighty leap of the imagination, as it were, and so did not recognize that their thoughts and ideas were dependent on the times in which they lived. Even worse, they hoped to transform the world piecemeal, in an evolutionary manner, by setting up communities independent of existing society, and so did not understand the forces or processes that governed historical development. In short, they did not understand history.

The 'scientific socialism' of Marx and Engels, on the other hand, was based on a 'correct' understanding of history in which the dominant ideas of an age were seen to derive from its 'material' conditions, especially the way it earned its living. Moreover, the phenomena of human society inevitably gave rise to their opposites, and history 'progressed' by the resolution of these opposites to create a completely new situation.

Like most historians, and, indeed, like Fourier, they recognized various stages of history, but maintained that 'the history of all hitherto existing society is the history of class struggles'. Thus the growth of capitalism, and, with it, the bourgeois class, inevitably gave rise to the co-operation and organization of the workers and the growth of the proletariat. This process increased the productive means of the society to the point where industry would be able to provide a high level of life and leisure for all, and thus there would no longer be any economic basis for a class society.

The antagonism between the bourgeoisie and the proletariat would be

resolved when the conditions were ready through a political revolution, followed by a prolonged period of reconstruction, called socialism, leading to a fully communist society. Communist society would be the first classless society of history, the state would have become mere administration, and life would be conducted according to the principle of 'from each according to his ability, to each according to his needs'.

Thus, according to scientific socialism, the activities of the 'utopians were doomed to failure, and, what is worse, were diversionary. When they set up communities or workshops in the belief that society would be gradually transformed, as dough by yeast, they were merely trying to circumvent history, and they diverted the proletariat from the important matters of economic and political struggle and political revolution'. This view explains the antagonism of Marx and Engels to any 'experiment' and to 'evolutionary' ideas about social change. The arguments that they practised on the utopians were later deployed with increased ferocity and intolerance towards anarchist communists such as Proudhon and Bakunin, and the dispute has left such a deep impression on Marxist politics that utopian speculation, however 'innocent', is virtually anathema to Marxists.

This chapter discusses the decentralized anti-state utopias of the libertarian and anarchist communists, some of the communities set up by them, and the treatment meted out to them by the disciples of scientific socialism. Finally there is the work of William Morris, whose political activity places him firmly between Karl Marx and the anarchists, but who shared the ideal of a decentralized stateless society and gave it its finest expression in his literary utopia–*News from Nowhere*.

Proudhon and Mutualism

Curiously, when Engels came over to England to look after his father's cotton mill, he seems to have been a communitarian socialist in the tradition of Robert Owen. While he was writing his *Conditions of the Working Classes in England* in 1844, he was also writing for Owen's *New Moral World* and for Fergus O'Connor's *Northern Star,* and in 1847 was defending O'Connor's land plan.

Top: The Stonebreakers by Gustave Courbet (1819–1877). In his choice and treatment of subject Courbet was strongly influenced by the philosophy of Proudhon
Above: The platform of the International Socialist Workers Congress, Zurich 1893. The French President Monsieur Carnot declared: 'We should have been happy to see on this wall by the side of our venerated Karl Marx the portraits of those great thinkers: Babeuf, Fourier, Blanqui, Saint-Simon; as also those of Robert Owen, Cesar de Paepe and other precursors of modern socialism'

Marx, however, was not at all taken with either Owen's communities or O'Connor's land plan, and it was his ideas that dominated the 40 years of collaboration with Engels which began in 1844. Thus in 1843 Engels could write about Pierre-Joseph Proudhon's first book — *What is Property?* — in the most favourable terms, but in 1848 Marx and Engels were classing Proudhon as a 'bourgeois or conservative socialist' alongside 'economists, philanthropists, humanitarians, improvers of the condition of the working class, organizers of charity, members of the society for the prevention of cruelty to animals, temperance fanatics, hole and corner reformers of every kind'. The split that had occurred still continues in communist ideas today, between those who wish to base a communist society on the centralized state, and those who assert that it must be a society of decentralized communities.

But for all the insults of Marx, Proudhon was 'the real inspirer' of French socialism and his influence can be seen in the founding of the First International, in the Paris Commune of 1871, in the co-operative workshops of the syndicalists, in the painting of Gustave Courbet and Camille Pissarro, and in the Russian *narodnik* (radical populist) movement. Indeed Tolstoy's novel *War and Peace* borrows many ideas on war and history from Proudhon. Proudhon answered his famous rhetorical question 'What is Property?', with the equally famous 'Property is Theft'.

However, he did not condemn all property, only that which was used to exploit other people without any effort on the part of the owner. On the other hand, the ownership of a dwelling, land, and tools that gave people effective control over their own lives, was the necessary keystone of liberty. In fact he criticized Owen and Cabet and their followers for removing this kind of property, the most important basis of individual freedom, and claimed that their kind of communism, rather than leading to

Below: Courbet's portrait of Pierre Joseph Proudhon (1809–1865) with his children. Proudhon's mutualist philosophy inspired a whole generation of French socialists

absolute equality, deformed equality by denying independent property. Thus he proposed a synthesis that eliminated the deficiencies of both, leading to a society of equality, justice, and independence.

Proudhon distinguished between different kinds of property, and claimed that a person should have absolute right over what they produce by their own labour, but no rights at all over the 'means of production'. According to his proposals, which he called *Mutualism,* society would be reorganized by means of free contractual associations of producers based on equalization of property, freedom of credit and the dissolution and irrelevance of the state. Moreover, he stressed the importance of economic co-operation and change in contrast to political activity. The social revolution, he wrote, is 'seriously compromised by a political revolution . . . the new socialist revolution will begin by the war of the workshops'.

Trusting that his war might be won without violence, Proudhon, like Winstanley, Godwin and even Cabet before him, also hoped to change society by the power of reason and example. Proudhon's image of a free society is decentralized and federal, based on association through contracts with workshops organized as co-operatives. The various workshop associations would be combined by contract into new industrial institutions that would replace government and the state to form what the later syndicalists called 'the social republic'. Again, relationships between associations should be governed by contracts:

> The idea of a contract excludes that of government . . . Between contracting parties there is necessarily a real personal interest for each . . . Between governing and governed, on the other hand . . . there is necessarily an alienation of part of the liberty and means of the citizen.

Proudhon's ideas found roots in many places in France during the ensuing years, but they found a permanent home in the Jura mountains of Switzerland. The watchmakers of the villages combined craftwork with farming, and treasured their independence. They 'associated' into a Fédération Jurasienne which fervently supported the ideas of Proudhon and Bakunin in all the struggles with Marx and Engels in the International Workingmen's Association. They were also very important in forming the ideas of the Russian Prince Peter Kropotkin, who visited the Jura in 1872 and met the printer, James Guillaume. 'We understand each other', he wrote. 'Guillaume warmly shook my hand and that afternoon was the beginning of our friendship. We spent all the afternoon in the office, he writing the addresses, I fastening the wrappers, and a French comrade who was a compositor, chattering with us all the while.' Later he met the basketmaker Benoit Malon and the watchmaker Adhemar Schwitzguebel, through whom he was able to meet other craftsmen at their work and attend the village meetings. Among them he found an independence of mind that he had not experienced elsewhere, and their example and ideas determined the main line of his anarchist philosophy.

Kropotkin and Mutual Aid

Although Kropotkin wished to stay in the Jura, Guillaume persuaded him that he was needed in Russia. He returned in May 1872 and joined the Chaikovsky Circle which was involved in educational propaganda and the circulation of radical literature. The Chaikovsky Circle was linked with the *narodniks,* in a 'To the People' campaign directed towards the huge Russian peasantry who had only just been freed from feudal serfdom. Kropotkin's writings in these two years developed the central ideas of his scheme. In *Should We Occupy Ourselves with Examining the Ideals of a Future Society?,* he recommends the possession of the land and factories by the producers themselves. Manual work was to be a duty for everyone; education should combine intellectual work and apprenticeship in a trade. There should be no state, and labour cheques could be substituted for money.

In 1874, along with many other *narodniks* Kropotkin was arrested,

Above: A craftsman from the Jura at work. Prince Kropotkin was impressed by the enthusiasm, harmony and democracy he witnessed amongst the mountain watchmakers and the small family workshops of the Jura. Here was the anarchist system in practice with independent local communities

interrogated, and imprisoned in the dreaded fortress of Peter and Paul in Leningrad. Two years later, he was transferred to another prison, and then to a prison hospital from which he was able to escape, via Finland, Sweden and Norway to Hull in England. From there he returned to the Jura, but eventually settled in London in 1886. During the 1890s his ideas became widespread through articles published in *Nineteenth Century* and *Freedom* and through his book *Fields, Factories and Workshops*.

He thought that society should be organized on the basis of communes, which would associate into a network of co-operations that would replace the state. But he diverged from the mutualism of Proudhon and Bakunin on the question of distribution and exchange. Where they had suggested a distribution system based on an individual's labour, Kropotkin rejected his own earlier idea of labour cheques as just another form of compulsion, and based distribution on need rather than volume of work.

> All things are for all men, since all men have need of them, since all men have worked in the measure of their strength to produce them, and since it is not possible to evaluate everyone's part in the production of the world's wealth. . . . If the man and the woman bear their fair share of the work, they have a right to their fair share of all that is produced by all, and that share is enough to secure their well being.

Such a system would depend on the attractiveness of work. Kropotkin believed that people were not naturally idle, and that if work was useful and freely undertaken in pleasant circumstances, then it would be satisfying in itself and also provide the usual satisfaction of working for the common good. In *Fields, Factories and Workshops,* he argued that it was folly for Britain to concentrate on industrial production to the exclusion of agriculture. He claimed, by statistical comparison with France, that she could double her food production by dispersing centralized industries and cities into local industrial and agricultural communities that would be as self-sufficient as possible. In such communities, reductions in the division of labour would lead to satisfying and creative work by enabling people to

Top: Victims of 'agricultural improvement' in the 1890s. Members of the newly formed Agricultural Workers Union after eviction from their cottage
Above: Prince Peter Kropotkin (1842–1921). A founding father of anarchism and communism, George Bernard Shaw described him as 'amiable to the point of saintliness'

use both their heads and their hands. Kropotkin's ideas had an immediate influence on utopian schemes and experiments in the 1890s, from Ebenezer Howard's *Garden Cities of Tomorrow,* to communities such as Stainthwaite and Norton, and the work of William Butler Yeats and Edward Carpenter.

By the time Carpenter invited Kropotkin to lecture in Sheffield, he had given up his work as a university extension lecturer and was combining agriculture and craftwork by growing vegetables and making sandals in the Cordwell Valley in Derbyshire. Although Kropotkin convinced him of the need for individual liberty in free association, his lifestyle owed much to the spirit of the American Henry David Thoreau. Writing in *Freedom* he called on his readers to desert the cities for the land in the way that Thoreau had done. Thoreau believed that materialism had led to an unnecessarily complicated and desperate way of life, and that people should return to the simple and the natural.

At Walden Thoreau found solace and tranquillity by submerging himself in the wilderness: 'This curious world we inhabit is more wonderful than it is convenient; more beautiful than it is useful; it is more to be admired and enjoyed than used.' Although his life at Walden resembled that of an ascetic, it was marked by an intense joy which derived from his belief that human life ought to be self-justifying in its happiness, not a duty or the means to an end. He found enough happiness and contentment through his empathy with the wilderness and the 'higher laws of nature' to recommend the life to the mass of humanity, and Carpenter, for one, believed that his book, *Walden,* was 'the most vital and pithy book ever written'.

Carpenter's advocacy of the natural life had effect in 1896 when Hugh Mapleton and Hubert Stansfield founded a community at Norton Hall, then owned by a retired lace manufacturer from Nottingham. The group was vegetarian, teetotal and non-smoking. They grew their own food and, like Carpenter, manufactured sandals that they sold from door to door in the surrounding neighbourhood. However, when their lease came to an end the community was broken up, some members joining the Stainthwaite group while others went into local government, the food inspectorate, industrial design, and the manufacture of vegetarian food.

Ruskin and The Guild of St George

Edward Carpenter and communities such as Norton, while directly influenced by the Russian Kropotkin and the American Thoreau, were also inspired by the earlier example of the Englishmen John Ruskin and William Morris. Ruskin, at the same time as Marx and many years before Kropotkin, had condemned the evil consequences of the division of labour. In *The Stones of Venice* of 1851 he wrote:

> We have much studied and much perfected, of late, the great civilized invention of the division of labour; only we give it a false name. It is not, truly speaking, the labour that is divided, but the man—divided into mere segments of men—broken into small fragments and crumbs of life; so that all the little piece of intelligence that is left in a man is not enough to make a pin, or a nail, but exhausts itself in making the point of a pin or the head of a nail. . . . We manufacture everything except men.

In 1871 Ruskin founded the Guild of St George to demonstrate that both the productivity of the land and the condition of the labourers could be improved through education. The work of the labourers would be strictly supervised by a hierarchy of elders, topped by the Master of the Guild. In April 1876, he agreed to lend £2,200 to the members of a Mutual Improvement Society in London to buy a thirteen-acre farm at Totley near Sheffield, on the understanding that they would manage the farm and repay the Guild in seven years. The members did not go to the farm themselves at first, but continued with their existing jobs and engaged two men to work the land. Nonetheless visitors flocked to see the experiment and a profitable sideline in refreshments grew up, while the farm produce itself was sold in Sheffield.

The project foundered over the issue of leadership and control, for, under the rules of the Guild, a master had been appointed, and his autocratic interpretation of his role led to the other members severing 'any responsibility for a connection with this farm'. Ruskin decided to turn it into an experimental farm for growing fruit trees in the north, but this too languished. By 1881 he wished to 'sell all that good-for-nothing land at Totley, and take somebody else in, for once—if we can—instead of always being taken in ourselves'. Eventually Edward Carpenter intervened and the farm was rented by a friend of his, George Pearson, who eventually bought it outright in 1929.

For all his problems with the Guild of St George, Ruskin made an enormous contribution to working-class education in England. Ruskin Societies were set up in many towns during the 1880s and eventually a Ruskin College was founded at Oxford University with funds from the Co-operative and Trade Union movements. The Liverpool Society had toyed with the idea of a community or agricultural colony as early as 1881, but nothing had come of it, because of a 'lack of conviction' among the members, as one of their number, J. C. Kenworthy, alleged. Kenworthy, however, pursued the idea, and became involved with plans of the 'Fellowship of the New Life' to set up communities and also with the English Land Colonization Society, who wished to establish colonies for those 'who were anxious to escape from the conditions of city life'. But whereas both these schemes were similar, in their paternalism and hierarchy, to Morgan's ideas of a Christian Commonwealth, Kenworthy thought more in terms of joint ownership and co-operative cultivation.

In 1890 he first came across the works of Tolstoy, and they filled the spiritual void that he had experienced with the other schemes. From then on Tolstoy's ideas became the dominant influence in his activities—from the founding of the Brotherhood Trust with Bruce Wallace in 1894 to his later utopian experiments.

Below: An expatriate Tolstoyan community in Bournemouth around 1900. Thousands of Russians and non-Russians became Tolstoy's passionate disciples and founded communities based on communal goods and ascetic living

Tolstoy and Peaceful Refusal

For Tolstoy, like Winstanley, Christ was a teacher who was found, not through an external mediator, but within the people themselves. Similarly his ideas about an imminent kingdom are similar to Winstanley's Third Age. His desire for a life close to nature, so clearly revealed in *Anna Karenina*, echoes Thoreau, and his image of a future based on self-government, co-operation and federated groups parallels that of his fellow Russian, Kropotkin. Tolstoy envisaged a future in which the state, the law and private property had been abolished by the force of a moral, rather than political, revolution. Government, he wrote, was organized violence to perpetuate slavery, and that could be abolished by abolishing government through reason, persuasion, example, and above all, by refusal to take part. Tolstoyans refused to co-operate in any way with the state, in police service, jury service, the payment of taxes, or any other work for the state. Inevitably this led them to set up communities within existing society, and many Russians and non-Russians attempted this road to the kingdom on earth.

One such colony began at Purleigh in February 1897 with only five people, but after only a year that had increased to 65, including J. C. Kenworthy, who had begun to build a house in the neighbourhood. But, while other Tolstoyan communities were being set up elsewhere in Britain, Purleigh itself fell into dispute and a group went to Whiteways, near Stroud in Gloucestershire. For three years they tried to practise complete communism and to farm the land together, but they found that the more committed and energetic members were doing the work of everyone else.

Moreover members who left tended to do so with the best clothes and any remaining money. Eventually they changed over to a system of individualism, and each member took up and cultivated their own plot of land, co-operating at the busy times of the farming calendar. Within months the more parasitic members had left for more 'co-operative' communities, leaving a small committed group. Thereafter the community thrived, although they never tried to reconstitute the 'pure communism' of the early period.

Meanwhile the Tolystoyan Brotherhood Trust had also broken up into factions, one of which went into printing, another into marketing (eventually merging with the London Co-operative Society), while the third formed the Brotherhood Church. It is ironic that this Tolstoyan communist group acted as host to the Fifth Congress of the Russian Social Democratic Party in 1903 at which the Bolshevik faction was born. Many of the major Russian revolutionaries were there, including Zinoviev, Gorki, Stalin and Lenin.

When the Bolsheviks came to power, they destroyed all the Tolstoyan or libertarian opposition in the few months following Kropotkin's death. Kropotkin had returned to Russia in 1917, and when he was buried in February 1921, his funeral procession was five miles long. The mourners carried black banners with 'Where there is authority there is no freedom' written on them in red. During the following month Trotsky and Zinoviev supervised the crushing of the Kronstadt rebellion, fomented by anarchists at odds with Bolshevik repression, and the secret police, the *cheka,* began murdering the imprisoned Tolstoyans. By the end of 1922 the libertarians were either silent, imprisoned, banished or dead, and the 'new intolerance' that Proudhon had warned of in his dispute with Marx had come of age, deepening the rift between libertarian and Marxist communists.

The *narodniks* and their sympathizers often combined hard heads and fertile imaginations. They numbered in their ranks some distinguished economists whose work is only now being analysed as seriously as it deserves. One such economist, Alexander Cheyanov, wrote in 1925 *The Theory of the Peasant Economy,* yet five years earlier had expressed, under a pseudonym, his hopes in a utopian dream called *The Journey of My Brother Alexei to the Land of Peasant Utopia.* Citizen Alexei Kremnev sleeps very deeply and wakes up in Moscow in 1984, but the world he sees is very different from that of George Orwell. In this new world, the Bolsheviks had lost power in 1934 because they were a new generation of 'barbarians who carried socialism to the limits of absurdity'. The 'era of

Below: Tolstoy Ploughing by Ilya Repin (1844–1930). For long periods his efforts to become a good farmer and improve the conditions of his peasants seemed a more urgent task than writing. 'The entire system of farming and, above all, the condition of the people as a whole must be transformed.' (Anna Karenina)

urban culture had passed away', a peasant labour party had come to power, industry had been relocated in the rural areas, there were no cities with more than 10,000 people except Moscow with 100,000, and the countryside was a chequerboard of peasant farms organized as co-operatives. Cheyanov was in prison during the Menshevik trial of 1931, but after that no certain record exists, except for the rumour that he was murdered in a Stalinist prison in 1939.

Morris and Reasonable Strife

William Morris, a man of prodigious energy and talent, exerted an influence on many fields, though he is best known today as a craftsman and designer. While at Oxford University during the 1850s, he himself was

influenced by the writings of John Ruskin, and shared with Ruskin many criticisms of industrial capitalist society. In particular they both saw the oppressed condition of the working class and the widespread ugliness of the environment and of industrial production as symptoms of the same disease – 'the curse of labour'. They believed that the problem of labour, of 'useful work' or 'useless toil' was at the root of problems both in society and in the arts.

For Ruskin, who had no experience of manual work, this led, as we have seen, to the founding of educational colleges for the working classes and the attempt to create a fulfilling working situation though a paternalist guild. For Morris, whose whole life was a search for useful and creative work, it led, eventually, to political agitation as a revolutionary socialist.

As a young man he tried his hand in architecture and as a painter, before settling down, in 1861, as jack-of-all-trades in the 'firm' that he had set up with his artist friends in the Pre-Raphaelite Brotherhood. They set out to make stained glass, furniture and household decorations at a standard of craftsmanship and design that would shame the shoddy standards of contemporary industry. Their success was such that the firm and Morris are considered by historians to be pioneers of modern art and design. Morris became the dominant partner, skilled in many trades, from weaving to dyeing, and in 1875 he took over and became the sole proprietor.

That year was something of a turning point in his life. He had become famous as the author of the *Earthly Paradise,* a retelling in verse form of the epic stories of the world. He also had a growing reputation as a craftsman and designer, he had passed through a prolonged crisis in his relationship with his wife, Jane Burden, the legendary beauty of the Pre-Raphaelite paintings, and, through his visits to Iceland and contact with its sagas, he had experienced a rebirth of hope that the state of the world might be bettered, a hope that had quite deserted him towards the end of the 1860s.

In 1875 Morris also joined the Liberal Party and began lecturing, mainly to middle-class audiences, on art, and, inevitably, work and the state of society. He argued that the general quality of art and manufacture

Above: William Morris (1834–1896). He was the author of News from Nowhere, which describes an ideal society after a socialist revolution
Below: A celebration of 'the triumph of labour' by Walter Crane who was a close friend of William Morris

reflected work conditions, and that good-quality products, that is, products with some love and care and art in them, could be made only by workers who were happy and fulfilled by what they did. Thus he urged his audiences to 'have nothing in your houses that you do not know to be useful or believe to be beautiful'. If they all did this, then the bottom would fall out of the market for shoddy goods and the manufacturers would be forced to improve the condition of their workers in order to improve the quality of their goods and so recapture their markets. Within a very short time Morris realized that his faith in the mechanism of the 'free market' was misplaced, so he began to consider the need for a complete change in the economic and class relationships of society.

The realization of this hope lay, he decided, in the creation of a socialist society. In 1883, at the age of 49, William Morris, famous craftsman, poet, manufacturer of artistic goods and widely tipped as the future Poet Laureate, joined a small revolutionary socialist group called the Social Democratic Federation, the first English Marxist party. Before long he was playing a major role, but in the following year was part of a group that broke away, with the support of Engels, to form the Socialist League.

The new party lasted into the 1890s, but Morris himself left in 1890 to form the Hammersmith Socialist Society. During these years he worked incessantly in the socialist movement, sold most of his library to support it financially and edited the League's paper *Commonweal*. *News from Nowhere* was first printed in weekly instalments in *Commonweal* in 1890, as a contribution to a discussion of the socialist future that had been stimulated by the publication, in 1888, of *Looking Backward,* a utopian romance by the American, Edward Bellamy.

Looking Backward is the archetypal state-socialist utopia. Its hero, Mr Julian West, a wealthy inhabitant of Boston, falls asleep amidst industrial chaos and competition in 1887 and wakes up to a world of regulation, order, equality and prosperity in the year 2000. According to Bellamy, by the end of the nineteenth century, the growth of monopoly had led to almost all economic activity being in the hands of just a few giant corporations. Eventually, through the agency of a 'National Party' and 'with absolutely no violence', this process had been carried to its logical conclusion, with production, distribution, research and everything else owned and controlled by a single nationalized corporation, the State. 'The epoch of the trusts had ended in the Great Trust.'

As a result, everyone now lived a 'cultivated' life, with equal material rewards for equal effort, and with sufficient variety of status to provide incentives for the most ambitious of men. Between the ages of 6 and 21, all have the advantage of equal and compulsory schooling, not only for their own benefit, but for 'the greater efficiency which education gives to all sorts of labour, except the rudest; [it] makes up in a short period for the time lost in acquiring it.'

At 21 the young ladies and gentlemen enter the industrial army where they work until the age of 45. Thereafter their life is their own, but it is only then that they are given the opportunity to vote for the holders of high office, such as the President of the United States, who is Commander-in-Chief of the industrial army, and his cabinet, the commanders of the main divisions or Guilds of the army. All other officers are appointed by the commanders on the basis of merit and hard work, and the higher one's position, the higher one's status.

For industrial soldiers in the ranks a grading system operates, reinforced by the publication of grading lists and the wearing of small but highly significant medals. Thus a powerful work-incentive is created, using honour and self-respect, and powerfully reinforced by pressure from the women, who, incidentally, form their own divisions of the labour army:

> Celibates nowadays are almost invariably men who have failed
> to acquit themselves creditably in the work of life. The woman
> must be a courageous one, with a very evil sort of courage,
> too, whom pity for one of these unfortunates should lead to
> defy the opinion of her generation—for otherwise she is free
> —so far as to accept him for a husband.

In fact for the ideal Boston of the year 2000, Bellamy reproduces, virtually unaltered, the values and expectations of an educated middle-class gentleman of the 1880s, but with a rationalized economy.

After three compulsory years in the 'dirty jobs' division of the army, people choose their trade or profession, with the co-operation of the bureaucracy who assess the manpower required in the various areas, and with the help of their superiors who report on their progress and discipline so far. For, of course, the industrial army is under military discipline, hence the fact that the members have no democratic rights.

> As for neglect of work, positively bad work, or other overt remissness on the part of men incapable of generous motives, the discipline of the industrial army is far too strict to allow anything whatever of the sort. A man able to duty, and persistently refusing, is sentenced to solitary imprisonment on bread and water till he consents.

Money no longer exists, but everyone has the same annual credit, regulated in various ways, to be used at the state-run stores, dining halls, washrooms and so on, and to pay rent for house, musical telephone, and the other necessities or luxuries of life. Domestic arrangements are the

Below: Ideal Government in the Country by the fourteenth-century Sienese artist Ambrogio Lorenzetti. This was a picture and subject dear to Morris. 'The secret of happiness', he wrote, 'lies in taking a genuine interest in all the details of daily life, (and) in elevating them by art . . .'

most modern and convenient, and housework has been banished by labour-saving furniture and decoration, electricity and public laundries and so on.

People eat either at home or in the public dining halls, where food is cheaper and of better quality. Each family has its own dining room set aside so they can have all the advantages of industrialized efficient cooking and service without the disadvantage of rubbing shoulders with all and sundry in a common hall.

The little details of Boston in the year 2000 are endless and ingenious, and a highly centralized industry brings a high material standard for all. But life has become broken up according to age into the three inflexible stages of learning, labour and leisure, and to live in Bellamy's state socialist utopia is to suffer from bureaucracy, competition and regimentation.

To Morris such a system was tyranny. He opposed state socialism, even though he considered that it 'would have this advantage over the individual ownership of the means of production, that whereas the state *might* abuse its ownership, the individual owners *must* do so'. *Looking Backward* showed some of the ways in which a state might abuse its ownership, but it was very popular for a while, selling nearly 200,000 copies within two years, and Morris felt that it was necessary to counter it. When he reviewed it in *Commonweal,* Morris wrote:

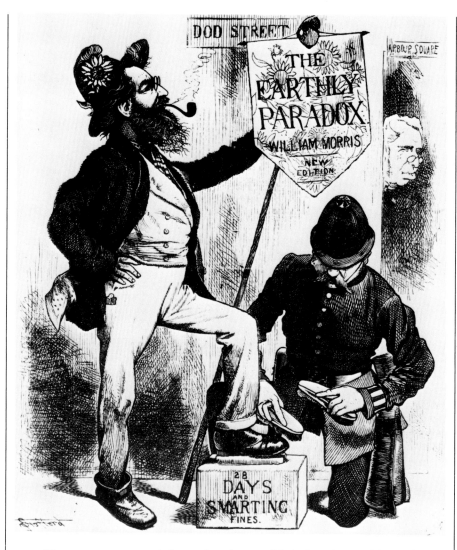

There are some socialists who do not think that the problem of the organization of life and necessary labour can be dealt with by a huge national centralization, working by a kind of magic for which no-one feels himself responsible . . . on the contrary, it will be necessary for the unit of administration to be small enough for every citizen to feel himself responsible for its details and to be interested in them; that individual men cannot shuffle off the business of life on to the shoulders of an abstraction, called the State, but must deal with it in conscious association with each other.

It is such a situation that Morris portrays in *News from Nowhere,* where, point by point, he up-ends the ideas of Bellamy. It is by no means a list and he is more concerned to portray the quality of personal life and relationships than administrative details, though there are details enough. But it was not just state socialism Morris had in mind: he was also writing within the anarchist/Marxist terms referred to above. While he broadly agreed with the anarchists on the eventual shape of an ideal state, he disagreed with the individualist and adventurist tactics of certain anarchists in the League.

The revolution, Morris thought, must be democratic and brought about by the will of the majority of the people, but it would, nonetheless, be violent, as it would inevitably be resisted by the remnants of the old ruling class. It would come when the time was ripe, when the workers were united and knew what they wanted, and when the capitalist class had become weak and no longer had the authority to control people's minds. In the long chapter on 'How the change came', Morris invents a chain of events to show the kind of process involved. Some of them would have seemed very familiar to his readers, as they were based on real incidents such as Bloody Sunday in 1887, when the police attacked a demonstration in Trafalgar Square and 200 people were badly injured and two died.

In *News from Nowhere* the change begins in 1952: through a prolonged economic crisis, tempered a little at first by state socialism, the country reaches such a crisis of inefficiency and collapse that capital can no longer make a profit, and workers cannot make a living. The government stands between capital and labour; the combined workers present a resolution to the government, but their demonstration is assaulted by police in Trafalgar Square. More demonstrations follow; a Committee of Public Safety is formed. Chaos ensues, food supplies dwindle, the Committee organizes requisitions, 'reactionaries' retaliate, government declares a state of siege and the army is called in. There is a lull before the storm, the army turns machine-guns on the next demonstration, the arrest of members of Committee and their acquittal on incitement charges by the jury follows. There is a period of dual government, the Committee grows in authority, the Party of Order takes over the government. The Committee is re-arrested. A General Strike is called, only socialist papers appear and they carry educational articles alone. The Committee is released and partially recognized. Right-wing vigilante groups are formed and finally civil war breaks out. By 1955 the war is over, and between them 'the two combatants, the workman and the gentleman . . . have destroyed commercialism'.

The reconstruction that followed was very different from what went before. People deserted the towns and invaded the country, so that the best of urban culture was mingled with the best of rural culture. Some towns, such as Manchester, disappeared altogether, and much of London was transformed into forests, farms and gardens. Central government,

'*When Adam delved and Eve span,*
Who was then the gentleman'
Left: *Edward Burne-Jones's design for the* Dream of John Ball *in which Morris wrote about the struggle for freedom in the Peasants' Revolt of 1381*

115

too, disappeared, and the country became a federation of self-governing communities in which politics as Morris knew it had ceased to exist.

Instead 'the whole people is the parliament', and the old Houses of Parliament found a new use as a convenient store for dung—'. . . not the worst kind of corruption, for fertility may come of that, whereas mere dearth came from the other kind, of which those walls once held the great supporters'. People kept in mind that the object of the revolution had been to 'make people happy', and this they mainly were, living their 'lives in reasonable strife with nature' rather than with an unreasonable struggle with each other.

But 'happiness without happy daily work is impossible', and work, instead of being reduced to a minimum, has a central position in Morris's utopia. Gradually people had learned to make and do things in enjoyable

Below: Work by Ford Maddox Brown. In a century that witnessed the degradation of work, radicals such as Proudhon, Marx, Tolstoy, Kropotkin and Morris stressed the value of useful work as the basis of a happy life

and satisfying ways, and they had stopped producing anything that demanded boring and painful work. To a great extent they turned from the machine to the hand, and the subsequent growth of craftsmanship led to a rebirth of art, so that work gave the double satisfaction of producing both utility and beauty. But technology is not discarded, simply developed to appropriate use, for instance in the boats that are driven by silent, smokeless 'force engines' and in the smokeless kilns, neither of which existed in 1890.

Work had become such a source of joy that people began to fear a work famine, and all strenuous, creative and useful activities from garbage collection to housekeeping are sought after and prized. They all take on a wide variety of work, and might travel many miles for the opportunity of a change of occupation, say from brain work to manual work. (Morris himself made a journey up the Thames from Hammersmith to Lechlade to take part in the haymaking). In general the traditional sexual division of labour operates, with women as weavers, gardeners, housekeepers and so on, and men taking heavier jobs such as ferrymen or stone masons. But much work is shared, especially seasonal agricultural work, and in any case, there is no rigid system.

For Morris the joy of work lies not in the unbridled pursuit of productivity, which leads to the manufacture of rubbish that people have to be duped into buying, but in taking a full interest in the daily necessities of life and elevating them by art. Happiness, that is, lies in making an art out of daily life.

As to the other arrangements of life, people generally live in separate family houses, though there is no marriage contract and no divorce court, and people think it absurd to try to regulate matters of affection by legislation. Morris feels that schemes such as Fourier's phalanstery were based more on a fear of poverty than on natural inclination, but nonetheless, each community has its guest house, with communal kitchens and dining rooms, and, as in everything else, there are no rules.

Similarly in education, people learn as and when they wish to:

> You expected to see children thrust into schools when they had reached an age conventionally supposed to be the due age, whatever their varying faculties and dispositions might be, and when there, with like disregard to facts to be subjected to a certain conventional course of 'learning'. My friend, can't you see that such a proceeding means ignoring the fact of *growth,* bodily and mental? No one could come out of such a mill uninjured; and those only would avoid being crushed by it who would have the spirit of rebellion strong in them. Fortunately most children have had that at all times, or I do not know that we should ever have reached our present position.

The people in *News from Nowhere* are recognizably human. Unlike the paragons of virtue necessary in most utopias, they have personal problems, there are grumblers and there is even killing. Like most violence, now that property is no longer an issue, it arises from problems of love, and as usual, is resolved within the community, without using any legal system.

Whereas Bellamy's hero had the doubtful good fortune of remaining in the state-socialist utopia, Morris awoke from his dream with the following message from the inhabitants of the ideal future:

> Go back and be happier for having seen us, for having added
> a little hope to your struggle. Go on living whilst you may,
> striving, with whatever pain and labour needs must be, to build
> up little by little the new day of fellowship, and rest, and
> happiness.

During the last years of his life, with his health failing, he did just this, working for co-operation between the socialist groups, and stressing the importance of 'making socialists', that is, people who knew what they wanted.

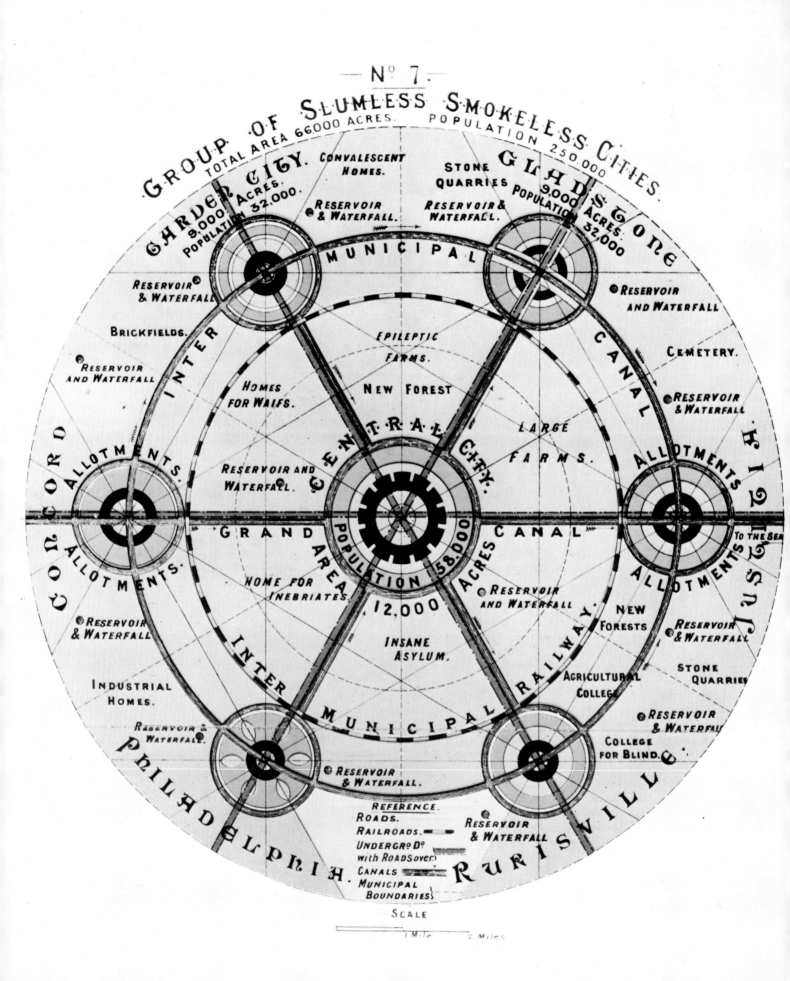

Official Utopias

Left: Diagrammatic layout from Tomorrow, a Peaceful Path to Reform by Ebenezer Howard. It shows the relationship of a 'garden city' to its surroundings

Many of the utopian schemes of the nineteenth century, from Morgan's Christian Commonwealth to Fergus O'Connor's land plan, had, at their heart, a belief in the regeneration of people and society through contact with the land. Owen, for instance, waxed long and poetic on the benefits to be gained by spade agriculture and the terrible damage done to the subsoil by the horse and the plough. A similar belief in the importance of contact with nature, can be found in the writings of Proudhon, Morris, Kropotkin, Tolstoy and Thoreau, and it is also found in the work of the American land reformer, Henry George.

His writings, particularly his *Progress and Poverty* of 1879, influenced many communities in the last years of the century, and in England they played a part in the early history of the Garden City Movement. George considered that the only way to remove the increasing poverty of industrial society was to make the land the common property of all.

Like Proudhon, he believed that people should have exclusive ownership of anything that they produced themselves. Thus they should be credited with any improvement that they made to the land, but this gave them no claim to the land itself, other than the equal share with every other member of the community in the value that is added by the growth of the community. However, George's solution was not the complete and immediate expropriation of the land into the commonwealth (that is, its nationalization), but the application of a single tax, which would 'appropriate rent by taxation'. In this way, the state would gradually become the effective universal landlord without calling itself as much. Through the operation of the tax, more land would become available for new buyers, the selling price of land would drop and land speculation would wither, but no one would be dispossessed.

Although the aim of common ownership of land was accepted by many different groups, the means of accomplishing it varied widely. The Land Nationalization Society, which was formed in London in 1882, contained those who wanted the state to buy the land and then rent it out to those who held it, those who wanted the state to nationalize without compensation and then manage it, and the supporters of George who rejected both compensation and management, but would have the state appropriate its annual value by taxation. These three different points of view could not co-exist for long, and the supporters of Henry George's ideas soon withdrew and organized themselves as the Land Reform Society.

Garden Cities of Tomorrow

The idea of regeneration through contact with the land is also found in the Garden City Movement which was founded soon after the publication of Ebenezer Howard's book, *Tomorrow: A Peaceful Path to Reform*. Although, like Robert Owen, he was always reticent about his influences, he was known to have been very impressed with George's *Progress and Poverty* and to have known the English Tolstoyans and the Fellowship of the New Life. However, he acknowledged that the initial stimulus came from Edward Bellamy's *Looking Backward*, though the garden city idea with its tendency to dispersed agricultural smallholdings is far removed from Bellamy's military version of an industrial state.

> When in 1898 a friend lent me *Looking Backward* . . . I was fairly carried away by the eloquence and evidently strong conviction of the author. I was led to put forward proposals for testing [Bellamy's principles] out though on a very much smaller scale – in brief to build by private enterprise an entirely new town, industrial, residential and agricultural.

The ideal diagram for a garden city was to build in a series of concentric circles with six boulevards radiating from the centre, very much as in the sketches for Washington by Major L'Enfant. In Howard's city centre, situated in a park, lay the civic buildings, with residential, shopping, commercial and industrial areas located in different parts of the city. The outermost circle was an agricultural belt which would supply the city with food. Howard proposed that an estate of 6,000 acres should be bought, of

The garden city idea was put into practice at Letchworth, Hampstead and Welwyn, with designs that varied from classical to medieval. Below: This is how a courtyard area in Hampstead was to look.
Above right: A view of Letchworth soon after construction, showing the extensive gardens which were intended to be both pleasant and productive
Right: Road and planting details to give the garden city feel, from Planning in Practice by Raymond Unwin

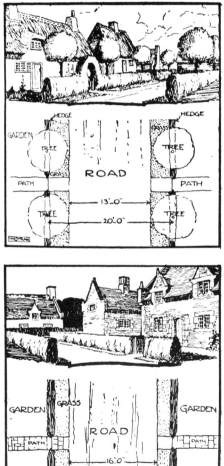

which the city itself would occupy only 1,000 acres, with a population of 30,000 people in the city and another 2,000 in the agricultural belt.

Each house was to occupy an average building plot of 6 metres (20 feet) by 40 metres (130 feet). Administration was to be by a Board of Management elected by the people paying rent. By forming building societies and co-operative businesses the citizens would not only build their housing, but contribute to the transformation of the society:

> The true remedy for capitalist oppression where it exists, is not the strike of *no work,* but the strike of *true work,* and against this last blow the oppressor has no weapon. If labour leaders spent half the energy in co-operative organization that they now waste in co-operative dis-organization, the end of our present unjust system would be at hand.

In other words the Garden City should push necessary productive work in the direction of workers' co-operatives and so build up the economic power of the workers themselves as against the capitalists.

In terms of the environment, Howard's aim was to create, in addition to the existing polar opposites of town and country, 'a third alternative, in which all the advantages of the most energetic and active town life, with all the beauty and delight of the country, may be secured in perfect combination'. The attraction of this 'town-country magnet', as he called it, derived partly from the environmental benefits, but also from there being 'one landlord—the community', and the possibilities for an industrial system based on co-operative principles, and a more equitable and just distribution of wealth.

On 10 June 1899, only eight months after the publication of his book, Howard attended the first meeting of the Garden City Association in the offices of A. W. Payne, the treasurer of the Land Nationalization Society. Indeed, nearly all of the 13 original members were involved with the community ownership of the land. By the end of the next year, Howard was able to boast that his scheme was so attractive that there were 'socialists and individualists, radicals and conservatives' involved.

In May 1900, Garden City Limited was formed with a share capital of £50,000, and with Thomas Adams as the first paid secretary. Conferences were held at Bournville in 1901 and Port Sunlight in 1902, both of which were pioneer communities founded by paternalist industrialists for their workforce. At the second conference a pioneer company was set up with the specific task of finding a site. However, there were no advocates of land nationalization on this board, and it is clear that the leadership of the association had passed, in three years, from advocates of popular co-operation and self-sufficiency to the advocates of benevolent paternalism. The new company bought nearly 40,000 acres from 15 different

Right: This publicity poster was designed to attract people to the new garden city at Welwyn, Hertfordshire. It contrasts the traditional industrial city and the modern suburb, and shows the garden city as a natural progression from them

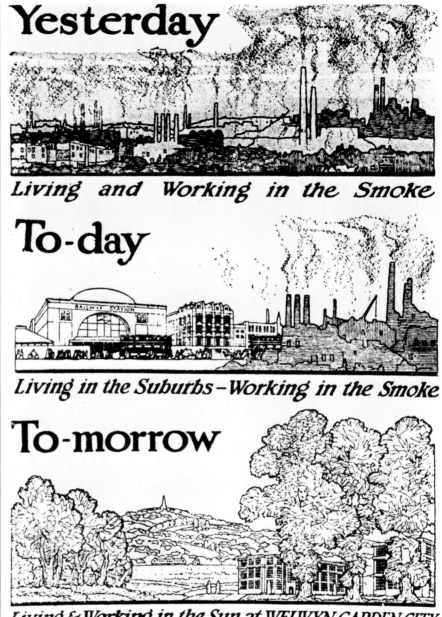

Yesterday
Living and Working in the Smoke

To-day
Living in the Suburbs – Working in the Smoke

To-morrow
Living & Working in the Sun at WELWYN GARDEN CITY

owners around Letchworth near Hitchin in Hertfordshire, and four years after the publication of Howard's book, the first garden city was opened.

The conferences of the early years show clearly the character of the movement and its basis in a moral critique of society. Adams, the secretary, wished to bring out the potential of the garden city idea for solving the deterioration he saw in the political and moral condition of the people, just as Owen had tried at New Lanark. Prophetically, he claimed that past attempts had failed because they had compartmentalized a general problem into the separate problems of overcrowding, rural depopulation and the depression of agriculture, which all contributed to a 'decline in the stature of the population'.

He believed that the development of cities had separated people from the 'good and controlling' influence of contact with the land, and recommended that as many of them as possible should return to contact with the land and the generation of their daily bread. 'The very foundation of our national prosperity is involved in restoring and maintaining the physique and moral character of the people of the country by getting more of them back to the land.'

The Garden City Movement, Adams believed, should increase its commitment to dividing as much land as possible into smallholdings, and the smallholdings themselves should be connected by a network of co-operatives for the buying and selling of produce. He also suggests a credit bank to help smallholders, and the establishment of small rural industries to provide part-time work.

It was ideas such as these, derived directly from anarchist utopians such as Kropotkin, that gave Letchworth its early character. Several members of earlier Tolstoyan communities went there, as well as former members of the Fellowship of the New Life. Ernest Rhys, a director of Dents, the publishers who had published Henry George's *Progress and Poverty,* also moved to the town and set up a printing works. People were attracted to a town that was intended to become 'a utopia of clean, pure air, flowers and perpetual sunshine'. A sketch of a typical male pioneer shows him clad in knickerbockers, with sandals on his feet. He is vegetarian, keeps two tortoises in his garden, a large photograph of the theosophist Madame Blavatsky over his mantlepiece and the works of Morris, Wells and Tolstoy on his bookshelves.

As the movement expanded, however, its aims became blurred and the moral fervour slowly evaporated leaving a residue of technical planning gimmicks. The movement changed from the advocacy of the garden city as a democratic co-operative community to the advocacy of open development, whether it was a 'garden' village, suburb, town or city. As a package

Left: The site plan of Welwyn Garden City, putting Ebenezer Howard's diagram into practice

of techniques it was adopted in the first Town Planning Act of 1909, and the garden city idea of moral regeneration degenerated into the ubiquitous dogma of British town planning. Like many utopian visions, it had provided a series of techniques, that were to become ends in themselves long after the original vision had been forgotten.

Planning the Future

The Garden City Movement, with its ideology of a return to the land and the ideal of a new co-operative community was just one of the influences that surrounds the emergence in the early years of this century of the new profession of planning. Others stemmed from the example of Germany in directing and stimulating economic and urban development through careful legislation, and in the health and hygiene concerns of the nineteenth century. Curiously, the latter too had its ideal community in Dr Benjamin Richardson's design for Hygeia in 1876.

The planning of towns and cities, that is the arranging of activities in space, is just one part of the more general task of planning the future of society, and the passing of the first Town Planning Act was an indication that, in a rapidly changing world, the future could no longer be left to chance. In such a situation, utopian thinking, projecting ideal images of the future, becomes commonplace and institutionalized. In pre-industrial societies people's way of life changed very slowly and radical change in the culture was literally unthinkable; besides there were always the paradise myths to fall back on if the present was particularly awful. They looked ahead and saw more of the same, whereas in a rapidly changing world no one can look ahead and seriously expect more of the same, or even business as usual. In a society which is consciously manufacturing the future, one way or another, 'future studies' is itself a growth industry, and the search for utopia is not only commonplace but obligatory.

Left: This impression of Hendon Garden Suburb shows how far the ideas of uniting work and home and being in contact with nature have been forgotten. There are no allotments to be seen, nature is ornamental, and the housing a dormitory for work elsewhere

Below: Ideal city of Hygeia. Whereas the garden city idea grew from social values, other planning ideas grew from the technical problems of managing large populations

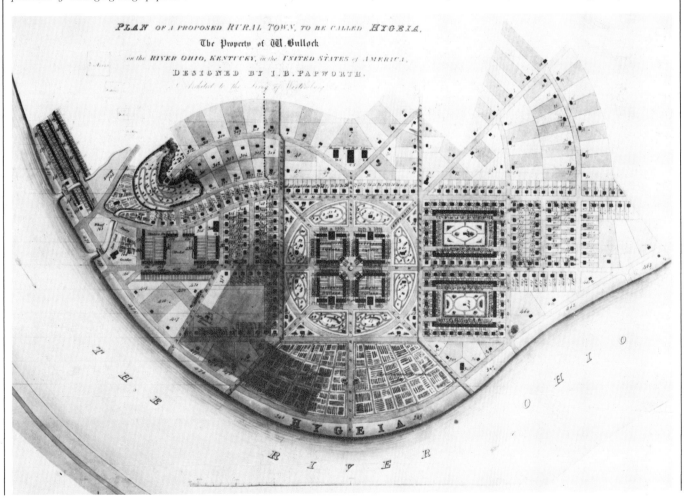

The Architect as Visionary

Left: During the twentieth century many architects and designers have created ideal images of the future, and some have played their part in trying to realize them. In particular, Vladimir Tatlin, shown here in a painting by Lissitsky (1890–1941), and the Russian Constructivists were faced with the vast problem of creating a new physical fabric for a different society

The utopian tradition of agricultural and craft communities managed, through the Garden City Movement, to influence and shape town planning and these agricultural and craft communities, like the garden cities, were a response to the various social, physical and moral evils associated with the industrial town or city. Utopians have almost always showed a concern for the shape of settlements, and the response to industrial capitalism of utopian community and garden city often concealed proposals to reform or replace industrial capitalism itself, as well as its city.

However, it was by no means apparent to everyone, particularly those closest to economic power, that the condition of the city was an indictment of the system, as Engels had argued so forcibly in his *Conditions of the Working Classes in England.* Rather, they said, the problem was that the traditional forms of settlement, for the most part organic and unplanned, were unable to accommodate the new economic social units—large factories, business districts, mass housing, railways, traffic and so on. Thus, they would argue, all that was needed was to find a new form or shape of settlement to fit the new content.

This search for the urban structure to fit the system is the main function of town planning, and it is the sad fate of most radical and utopian proposals that they have provided the ideas and techniques that have been used for the maintenance of the system rather than its transformation.

Just as the utopians projected a vision of the future, so do the planners, and in the same way their visions make assumptions about human nature, equality, happiness, fulfilment and work. A city planned with separate high-income and low-income housing areas, industrial estates and a stock exchange is just as much a model for a class society with production ruled by capital, as Campanella's City of the Sun is a model for a society that values learning and is guided by a priesthood. Some planners have envisaged mixing different social classes, but in a class-ridden society, their plans are doomed to failure.

Most planning proposals and techniques can be traced back to some utopian scheme, either directly as in the case of Ebenezer Howard, or by way of a symbol that has become part of the sacred lore of the planners, 'the professional utopians'. The 'open space' that appears on the redevelopment plan is not really a windswept boggy patch of uneven grass, barely covering the rubble of some dwelling or cornershop; rather it represents the 'sun', 'light' and 'air' of Corbusier's *Radiant City* or the semi-rural, folksy splendour of *Garden Cities of Tomorrow*.

Several architects have contributed to these ideas and symbols. Although their work takes the form of physical plans, these schemes for the twentieth-century ideal city are no less descriptions of a future utopian world than were the literary utopias of previous centuries, and, like them, they are frequently seen as guides to action. For the most part they accept the notion of the city (for, of course, the architect as we know him is almost an invention of the city and could not exist without it), but they all seek to rationalize and transform it according to a theme, whether it be socialism, 'authority', communism, mass production, automation, mobility or merely the 'affluent society'.

La Cité Industrielle

In 1899, Tony Garnier, a student at the Beaux Arts School of Architecture in Paris won the coveted Rome Scholarship which gave him five years of study at the Villa Medici at Rome. After the first year his proposed design, for an ideal industrial city, was rejected by the Beaux Arts as an unsuitable topic for academic study, but he continued with it anyway, and in 1904 the scheme was exhibited in Paris. *La Cité Industrielle* was later published in 1917, and had Garnier been as ambitious a self-publicist as some later

Below: Tony Garnier (1868–1948) designed the Cité Industrielle between 1898 and 1904
Bottom: This panorama of his city shows the public and administrative buildings

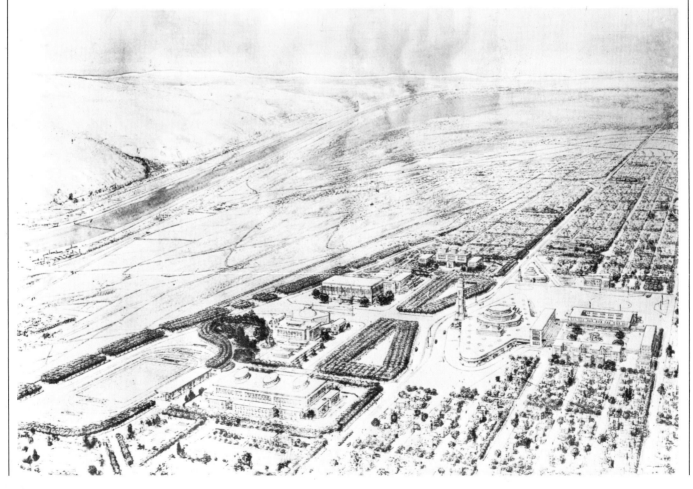

128

Above: This residential area in the Cité
Industrielle has shared public gardens
between the houses

architects, it might well have provided the model for planning in this century. As it was, Garnier became city architect for Lyon, and although he built many buildings that are strikingly similar to those in *La Cité Industrielle*, the scheme itself did not become widely known outside the circle of architects.

The city is designed 'realistically' in the sense that it is related to natural topography and resources, and assumes contemporary agriculture, industry and technology. Situated in a landscape such as one might find in the South of France, and linked to an existing old town, it has water available for hydro-electric power, and access to coal, mineral resources and to a river. It has links with a national rail and road system, and the buildings themselves are in reinforced concrete, which was then a relatively new material, and the designs are eminently buildable.

However, instead of the jumble of functions of the nineteenth-century city, relieved perhaps by some grand boulevards, the Cité Industrielle is zoned into three main areas. There is an administrative area adjacent to the old town, with the railway station linking the two, an industrial zone between the administrative centre and the river, and a residential area surrounding a cultural and sports centre. Schools, in which boys and girls receive the same education, are distributed among the housing, and the city has several hospitals situated on higher ground.

Instead of the tension and competition of the old cities, Garnier presents an image of order and relaxation, but it is by no means a rigid or brutal order. He has assumed that a socialist revolution has taken place (based on ideas from Proudhon and Saint-Simon), and made coherent logical planning possible. 'Distribution of land, everything related to distribution of water, bread, meat, milk and medical supplies, as well as the reutilization of refuse will be given over to the public domain.' Moreover, he assumes that 'a certain progress in social order' has resulted in 'an automatic adoption of rules for road use, hygiene etc., so that actual laws are not necessary'.

The city contains no lawcourts, prisons, churches or police stations

Above: A view over the city shows the port, factory areas, railway station and, in the distance, the dam for hydro-electric power

because the new society, governed by socialist law, would have no need of churches, and, with the passing of capitalism, there would be no more thieves, cheats or murderers either. But there are several assembly halls of varying sizes, including 'an open-air assembly centre for 3,000 people, to be used for meetings and for listening to gramophone records of music, and for parliamentary debates . . . and a large number of small meeting rooms for societies, syndicates and various other groups'.

Garnier's city has all the facilities to be expected in the modern city—concert halls, museums, libraries, exhibition halls, sports centres, swimming pools, public baths, fire stations, health centres and hotels—all publicly owned, and open to everyone. One of the most striking aspects of the Cité Industrielle drawings is that they are inhabited: they show a concern for people, not just for buildings. The city is not so much a rational industrial plan, but the context for a leisured, healthy, cultured, co-operative and democratic way of life for its 35,000 inhabitants. It tries to show that alienation and ugliness are not the inevitable consequence of industrialization, and that the 'modern world was not incompatible with urban grace'. However, whereas Garnier sought to banish the alienation of the city, the Futurists in Italy seem to have been inspired by it.

Antonio Sant'Elia and the Futurist City

The Futurist movement was founded, propagated and financed by the rich Italian poet, Filippo Marinetti. In an Italy that was rediscovering a national consciousness after four centuries of domination by foreign powers, he gathered around him a group of writers, and artists, who combined in an explosive attack on traditional culture and institutions. They proposed the total physical annihilation of traditional Italy, to allow the emergence, through 'universal dynamism'—'the absolute life force of matter'—of a new modern, industrial and pioneering Italy.

Futurism is characterized by cults of speed, youth, movement, excitement, danger, aggression, turbulence, noise, energy and chaos. 'The world's splendour has been enriched by a new beauty: the beauty of speed', wrote Marinetti in the *Foundation Manifesto* of 1909.

> There is no more beauty except in strife. No masterpiece without aggressiveness. Poetry must be a violent onslaught upon the unknown forces, to command them to bow before man. . . . Time and space died yesterday. Already we live in the absolute, since we have already created speed, eternal and ever present. We wish to glorify war—the only healthy giver of the world— militarism, patriotism, the destructive arm of the anarchist, the beautiful ideas that kill, the contempt of woman. We wish to destroy museums, the libraries, to fight against moralism, feminism, and all opportunist and utilitarian meanness.

The Futurists particularly disliked the traditional cities: Venice, Florence, and Rome were 'three festering sores', but they praised modern cities like Milan, and immersed themselves in the fragmented and transient sensations and experiences of city life.

> We shall sing of the great crowds in the excitement of labour, pleasure and rebellion; of the multicoloured and polyphonic surf

Above: A building study for a Futurist city by Sant'Elia, their premier architect who was killed in World War I. Futurism was characterized by cults of speed, youth, movement, excitement, danger, aggression, turbulence, noise, energy and chaos
Left: Brawl in the Galleria by Umberto Boccioni (1882–1916). He captured the spirit of Futurism as set out in their 1910 Manifesto, to which he was a signatory

The vast scale of Sant'Elia's buildings in the ideal Futurist city (right and below) contrasts violently with the human scale of Garnier's Cité Industrielle. Most of the drawings were untitled and it is unclear what these massive buildings were intended for

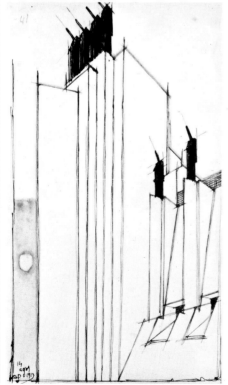

of revolutions in modern capital cities; of the nocturnal vibrations of arsenals and workshops beneath their violent electric moons; greedy stations swallowing smoking snakes; of factories suspended from the clouds by their strings of smoke; of bridges leaping like gymnasts . . . of broad-chested locomotives prancing on the rails like huge steel horses.

The industrial revolution had arrived relatively late in Italy, and in the first decade of the twentieth century the new industrial centres of the north had mushroomed from practically nothing. Production in most industries had trebled, and new industries were begun, including the motor industry with whose products the Futurists were so infatuated. With all this came nationalist ambitions, for freedom from the influence of Austria, and for colonial possessions. The Futurists themselves were intensely nationalistic; the writer Papini wrote that he had become a Futurist because 'Futurism means Italy, an Italy greater than the Italy of the past, more modern, more courageous, more advanced than other nations'. They saw freedom from Italy's cultured past as part and parcel, if not the prerequisite, of the political freedom and industrial supremacy they campaigned for.

It is in Italy that we launch this manifesto of violence, destructive and incendiary, by which we this day found Futurism because we would deliver Italy from its canker of professors, archaeologists, cicerones and antiquities . . . we would free her from the numberless museums which cover her with as many cemeteries. . . . Set fire to the shelves of the libraries! Deviate the course of the canals to flood the cellars of the museums . . . for art can be nought but violence, cruelty and injustice.

Marinetti directed a provocative artistic and political campaign, with manifestos, lectures, poetry readings, demonstrations, and physical attacks on critics. He arranged 'Futurist evenings', and probably the fighting with which they usually ended. On one occasion he dropped 80,000 leaflets from the tower of St Mark's in Venice calling for the destruction of the palaces, the filling-in of the canals, and the transformation of the city with motorways and factories. All of this made excellent publicity, and after World War I, Marinetti was able to put his organizing experience and talents to appropriate use in the service of Mussolini.

Although the literary and artistic imagery of the Futurists was inspired by the industrial city, it was not until 1914 that Marinetti gained the recruit capable of creating a Futurist architecture. This was Antonio Sant' Elia, who was introduced to Marinetti after exhibiting a series of drawings for a 'New City'. Although he held many similar, though more restrained ideas, Sant'Elia was nevertheless a reluctant Futurist, and the eventual *Manifesto of Futurist Architecture* has been extensively reworked by Marinetti. The ideal Futurist city was to be a place of constant movement and change, continually being demolished and rebuilt.

Houses have a shorter life span than we do; every generation will have to build its own city . . . we must invent and rebuild *ex novo* our Modern City like an immense and tumultuous shipyard, active, mobile and everywhere dynamic, and the modern building like a gigantic machine. Lifts must no longer hide away like solitary worms in the stairwells, but the stairs — now useless — must be abolished, and the lifts must swarm up the facades like serpents of glass and iron. The house of cement, iron and glass, without carved or painted ornament, rich only in the inherent beauty of its lines and modelling, extraordinarily brutish in its mechanical simplicity, as big as need dictates, and not merely as zoning rules permit, must rise from the brink of a tumultuous abyss; the street which, itself, will no longer lie like a doormat at the level of the thresholds, must plunge stories deep into the earth, gathering up the traffic of the metropolis connected by necessary transfers to metal catwalks and high-speed conveyor belts.

Below: Tatlin (1885–1953?) and his colleagues working on the model for a 'Monument to the Third International', 1919–1920. Tatlin's design, though unbuilt, has provided the characteristic image of the Constructivist movement

The Città Nuova was presented in a series of perspective drawings, with little indication of function and none of planning. Like all Futurist products they are concerned with sensations. The city existed for the aesthetic stimulation of an artistic élite, who made a cult of competitive chaos and had neither contact nor empathy with the 'masses' who had to live with it — they too, were part of the spectacle. Futurist rhetoric might be gloriously exhilarating, but for the underlying seriousness of it all. The fact that mechanization had made machines out of people was not, for them, a matter of regret but of rejoicing, and alienation is welcomed as the source of a new sensibility.

When the World War I broke out, several Futurists, true to their conception of war as the ultimate cleansing agent, volunteered, and Sant' Elia, Marinetti and the painter Boccioni went into a cycle battalion. Sant'Elia is reputed to have amused himself at the front by building Futurist architecture in ice and snow. But, war being no respecter of talent, both Sant'Elia and Boccioni were killed in 1916. Sant'Elia was only 28 years old. Marinetti, the survivor, returned home, but Futurism as a movement did not revive. It left a political and social legacy that contributed, through its leader and idealogue, to the growth of Fascism, and Marinetti fostered Sant'Elia's reputation in the hope that his work might be the foundation for a Fascist architecture. However, the drawings have

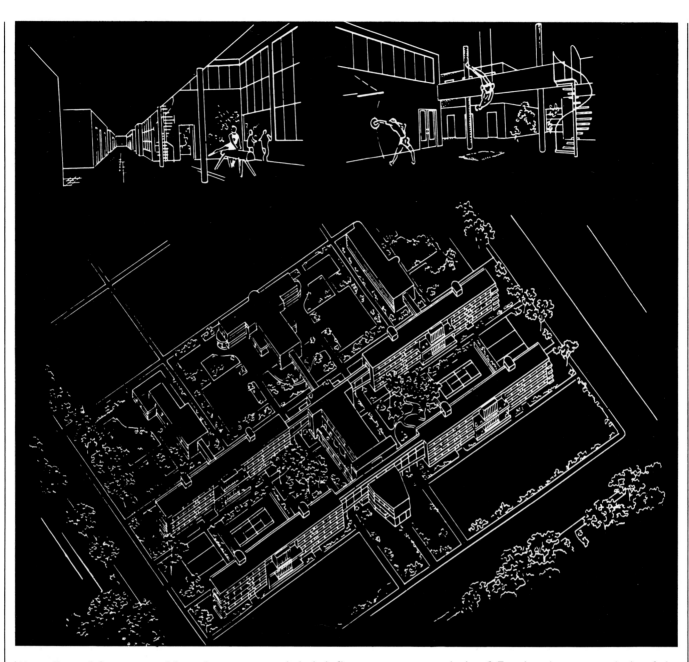

Above: Proposal for a communal house for Kuznetsk, 1930, by Alexander and Leonid Vesnin. Apartments are in the wings with communal facilities in the centre

exerted their influence not as symbols of Fascism but as symbols of the 'machine age' and Sant'Elia's images have haunted devotees of high technology to the present day.

Revolutionary Constructivism

World War I reshaped the political map of Europe and left all the participants with major problems of social and environmental reconstruction. In Russia, the October revolution had opened up enormous new possibilities, which found expression in the projects of the Constructivists. But, for the most part, the projects remained on paper, for Russia was divided by civil war, isolated from the rest of the world, and its industrial base, never extensive, had been virtually destroyed in the prolonged conflict. Soviet Constructivists designed for anything and everything that might have bearing on the construction of a communist society, from workers' clothing by Rodchenko, and agit-prop posters by Lissitsky, to the monument to the Third International by Tatlin.

This vast spiral tower, taller than the Eiffel Tower, was to be functional as well as symbolic. It contained three chambers, one above the other. 'By means of special machinery they are to be kept in perpetual motion but at different speeds.' The lowest chamber, for legislative purposes, a cube, was to turn on its axis once a year. The chamber above this, a pyramid, made one revolution a month, and was for meetings of assemblies and executive bodies. Finally the third and highest part, a cylinder, turned on its axis once a day and would be used chiefly for administration and propaganda, with a bureau of information, for newspapers, manifestos, telegraphs, radio apparatus and cinema projectors, forming a kind of early multi-media communications centre. The diagonal spiral of the enclosing structure is intended to be the 'symbol of the modern spirit of the age'.

Constructivism was not just a matter of monuments. With all the chaos and hardship surrounding them, architects were faced for the first time with the real problem of socialist building on a massive scale, not just a utopian project. The problem of the ideal communist city preoccupied Russian architects throughout the 1920s. Their work parallels that of Le Corbusier in France, with 'rational' zoned cities designed for industrial production, assuming a homogeneous proletariat, and using analogies of industry for their layout, and involving the mass production of building components.

Lenin's dictum that 'Communism equals soviets plus electricity' meant that for the Constructivists, Soviet architecture was 'based on the specific features of a new *social* type' as well as 'technically perfect construction methods'. They produced many projects for workers' clubs, educational institutions, and community buildings with dining halls, communal kitchens, nurseries and washrooms. They recognized the importance, both for a communist society and a functionally zoned and fragmented city, of the buildings that brought people together, the 'social condensers' as Lissitsky called them. Few projects were completed, however, and when Russia did start rebuilding it was not to Constructivism that Stalin turned, but to the solid, enduring, overscaled impressive neoclassicism so loved by usurpers of power.

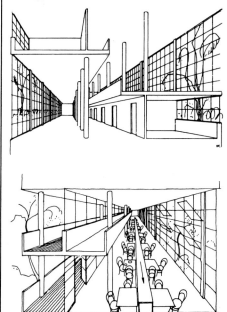

Below: Perspective sections through a communal house by Barsch and Vladimirov, 1929, showing individual rooms and automated communal dining area
Bottom: Bruno Taut (1880–1938) used glass buildings as centrepieces in his utopian designs

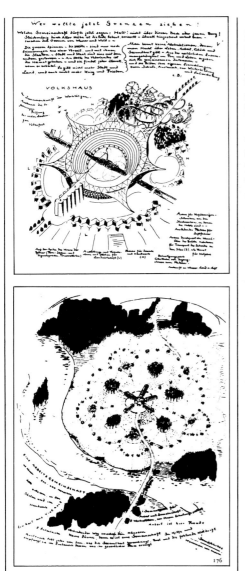

Above: Illustrations from 'The Dissolution of the City' by Taut (1920): a community centre (top); and a working community for between 500 and 600 people, living in 100 houses around a glass central building (above). He hoped to reproduce, in glass, the mystical and transcendental qualities of natural crystalline forms

The City of Glass

In Germany, the immediate postwar period was almost as turbulent as in Russia, with the possibility that Germany too might have its revolution, though the regional socialist governments that were set up were soon destroyed. In the political confusion, postwar reconstruction was difficult, and the problems were made worse by the crippling war reparations imposed by the allied powers in the Treaty of Versailles.

Artists and architects, with everyone else, contributed to the debate, or rather the struggle for people's bodies and minds, with programmes, manifestos, symbolic and utopian designs, practical building and educational proposals. In March 1919 the 'Works Council for Art' published their manifesto in Berlin. 'Art and the people must form a unity', they proclaimed. 'Art shall no longer be the enjoyment of the few but the life and happiness of the masses,' and they must aim at an alliance of all the arts 'under the wing of a great architecture'. It all sounded very much like a polemical version of William Morris, but the Works Council for Art also proposed that 'people's housing' should be the 'means of bringing all the arts to the people', whereas Morris would have the people working in freedom, producing their own art, and coping with their own housing.

In the following month, Walter Gropius, one of the leaders of the Berlin group, took over the now famous Bauhaus School of Art and Design, the pioneering college in modern design and architecture. As part of the curriculum he called for the 'mutual planning of extensive utopian structural designs—public buildings and buildings for worship—aimed at the future'. At the same time he was participating with the architect Bruno Taut and others in circulating *Utopian Letters,* also exploring possible futures.

Taut, the inspirer of the group, propagated and popularized many of the ideas that preoccupied expressionist artists and architects, particularly through four books published between 1917 and 1920: *The City Centre, (Die Stadtkrone), The Dissolution of the City (Die Auflösung der Städte), The World Architect (Der Weltbaumeister),* and *Alpine Architecture (Alpine Architektur).* The last was dedicated to Paul Scheerbart, whose *Glass Architecture* was a major expressionist influence.

Glass, for Scheebart, had mystical and transcendental qualities, including the power to transform the world and generate a new morality. 'A person who daily sets eyes on the splendours of glass', he wrote *'cannot* do wicked deeds'. Most of Taut's projects have glass buildings as centre pieces, either as temples or community centres, and *Alpine Architecture* literally presents translucent crystalline inspirations to virtue on a massive mountainous scale. But Taut's ideas are not always complementary, and in his two books on the ideal city he proposes opposing solutions.

The first has centralized cities with layouts similar to that of Ebenezer Howard, only far larger. His cities with half a million inhabitants, were about 15 times the size of a garden city. In contrast, *The Dissolution of the City* attempts a specific utopian proposal. He presents the world as it might appear transformed according to the ideas of Kropotkin, with no state. He imagines decentralized, self-sufficient communities, each with their own industries housed in small workshops, with solar-generated electric power. Everyone is involved in both industrial and agricultural work, and everything is managed according to the principles of mutual aid . . . with a little help from glass.

The Model 'T' Democracy

Decentralization, for instance, is often associated with the overturning of capitalism and the reversal of contemporary industrial and economic trends, but it is not always so. For the American architect, Frank Lloyd Wright, the dispersal of the population was the prerequisite for individuality and democracy, and he had his own somewhat poetical versions of what these were. 'Individuality', said Wright, 'is the fundamental integrity of the soul of man,' and 'Democracy is the very gospel of Individuality'. What this means in practice is that 'when every man, woman and child may be born to put his feet on his own acres, and every unborn child finds his acre waiting for him when he is born—then democracy will have been realized'. Thus in Broadacre City, 'the city of the new freedom', Wright has the inhabitants dispersed across the land on one-acre plots. But where the communists and anarchists have their populations dispersed into small self-sufficient communities, in Broadacre they are dispersed as separate nuclear families. His families practise subsistence farming, keep a cow, but still have the advantages of the modern city at hand, including the chance to work in a factory. For Wright retains all the benefits of the city and private enterprise industry, linking them all up with the wonders of modern transport, on the principle that transport technology, particularly the car, has shrunk time and distance, making the concentration of people in cities unnecessary as well as unhealthy and undemocratic. In Broadacres,

> any citizen may choose any form of production, distribution, self-improvement, enjoyment, within the radius of say, ten to forty minutes of his own home—all now available to him by means of private car or plane, helicopter, or some other form of fast public conveyance . . .

Rather than a city in any conventional sense, Broadacres is a grid of homesteads, facilities and factories within a huge network of transportation. Individualism, and the American pioneering tradition, in which people have independence and self-esteem through labour on their own land, is combined with modern industry, in which mass-production demands a workforce to man the factories. Thus Broadacres is the motorized American dream, and in its design Wright has reconciled his intense belief in the individual with his equally intense belief in the inestimable benefits brought to mankind by the assembly lines of Henry Ford.

But Broadacre City, like many of the utopian schemes of the nineteenth century, is also a programme for the relief of the poor. Wright saw urban poverty as a product of property speculation, and the poor were 'those citizens damaged by inexorable multiple *rents*'. His remedy is bracingly simple; just move the poor to their own plot of land, with a subsidy if necessary, and they will build a minimal dwelling, gradually extend it, buy a second-hand car, grow a little food, work in the factory, gain self-esteem, and suddenly, hey presto, they are poor no more. Meanwhile the fortunes of the city speculators have justly dwindled, while those of the industrialists have prospered. It is this aspect of Broadacre City that has led some critics to treat it as a motorized version of Owen's 'parallelogram of paupers' or Minter Morgan's Christian Commonwealth. The whole scheme would be impossible without the motor car. The dispersed nature of the city makes its possession essential, but to possess it the worker must supplement the food from the one-acre plot by a cash wage, earned by working in a factory, presumably making the cars that are essential to living in the city.

Broadacre city is not just an ingenious scheme to get workers into factories without driving them off the land, it is Wright's ideal for an organic life for all—self-sufficient, close to nature, free and democratic—'our free city for the sovereignty of the individual . . . the nature of democracy when actually built'. It is also peculiarly American in that it assumes wide open spaces for the urban population to expand into—in 1932 Wright calculated that there were 57 acres of good 'green' land per person in the USA.

Such an idea was impossible in Europe, where land was relatively in short supply, and large-scale industry and the city were inextricably linked. Unless, like Kropotkin, one was prepared to disperse industry too, and hence lose the magical benefits of mass-production and profit, then the only solution lay in the rationalization of the city, not in its dissolution. No one contributed more to this discussion than Le Corbusier, and the ideas that he developed in the 1920s became the new doctrine of modern architecture and planning when they formed the basis of the 'Athens Charter' of the International Congress for Modern Architecture, 1933.

Below: This detail of an apartment façade is from Le Corbusier's scheme for a city for three million inhabitants (1922)

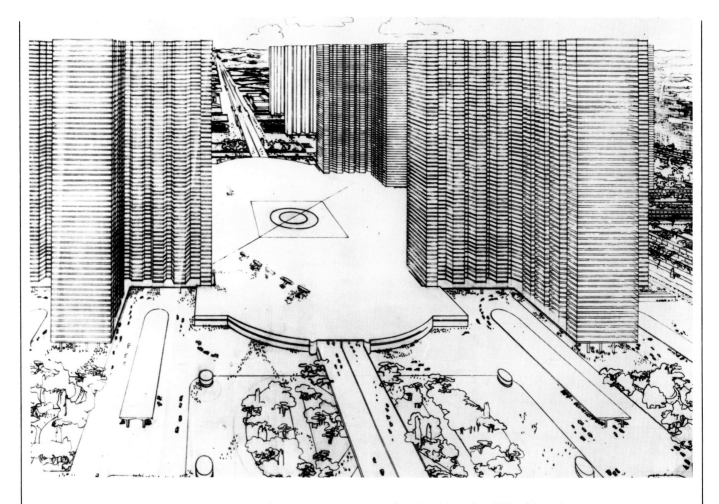

Above: City for three million. This view shows the central station and airport with adjacent office buildings

A Machine for Working in

In 1920 Le Corbusier had published *Towards a New Architecture (Vers une Architecture)* in which he had called for a modern architecture appropriate to the 'machine age'. Buildings should be designed in a modern and functional way just as ships, racing cars, lorries and aeroplanes were. 'A chair', he wrote, 'is a machine for sitting on'. Similarly, 'a house is a machine for living in'. Houses, like cars, should be mass-produced, standardized industrial products, rather than one-off objects, laboriously and inefficiently put together outside in all weathers. He also argued that the 'question of building is at the root of the social unrest of today', because he believed that everyone had a 'primordial instinct' for shelter and the various social classes no longer had dwellings 'adapted to their needs'. The choice was 'Architecture or Revolution'.

This was certainly a magnificent way to sell an architectural programme, with political unrest throughout Europe and the example of the Russian revolution fresh in people's minds, and it was inevitable that he should apply himself to the problem of the city. This he did in 1922 on a massive scale, in his project for 'a contemporary city for three millions', which contains most of the ideas later developed in *The Radiant City*.

Just as a house is a machine for living in, so 'a town is a tool' for an ordered, stratified, efficient, modern life, provided for people who are fully adapted to industrial society. A city is 'the grip of man on nature,' he said, 'a human operation directed against nature, a human organism both for protection and for work'. Its characteristic was 'order', represented in geometry, and the straight line as well as the functional separation of its parts.

> Man, by reason of his very nature, practises order . . . his actions and thoughts are dictated by the straight line and the right angle . . . the straight line is instinctive to him and his

mind apprehends it as a lofty object . . . he walks in a straight line because he has a goal and knows where he is going . . . the modern city lives by the straight line, inevitably; for the construction of buildings, sewers and tunnels, highways and pavements. The circulation of traffic demands the straight line: it is the proper thing for the heart of the city. The curve is ruinous, difficult and dangerous; it is a paralysing thing. The straight line enters into all human history, into all human aims into every human act . . . geometry is the foundation . . . the material basis on which we build those symbols which represent to us perfection and the divine. . . .

Le Corbusier was very fond of the straight line at this stage of his career, seeing it as the inevitable and symptomatic result of machine production, and its use as a symbol of civilization.

Orthogonal (right-angled) planning was as significant to him as concentric circular plans had been to Campanella when he designed the City of the Sun as an analogy of the solar system. Where Campanella has a temple and observatory in the centre, the centre of the highly civilized city for three million contains the administrative and commercial district. Its 24 gigantic cross-shaped skyscrapers 'contain the city's brains, the brains of the whole nation'.

They stand for all the careful working-out and organization on which the general activity is based. Everything is concentrated in them: apparatus for abolishing time and space, telephones, cable, wireless, the banks and business affairs, the control of industry, finance, commerce, specialization.

Below: In the 'Plan Voisin', Le Corbusier applied the techniques of the city of three million to Paris (1925)

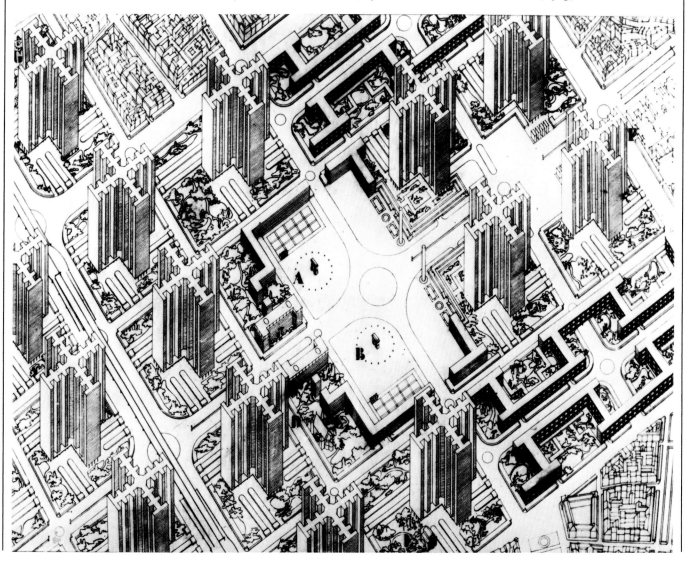

However, in the very heart of the city, the altar of the temple as it were, lies the multi-level traffic interchange, containing motorways, railway station, bus station, and on top, between the skyscrapers, an airport. All of this expresses the importance and virtue of speed and mobility in the modern city. 'The city of speed', Le Corbusier wrote, 'is the city of success'. Adjacent to the administrative areas lies a cultural and civic centre in its own park. Both are surrounded by the housing zone.

Le Corbusier felt that the skyscraper was not really appropriate for family life, and that 'its internal economy demands so elaborate a system that if one of those structures is to pay, only business can afford the cost'. The family should have all the benefits of sun, light and air, greenery, privacy, vistas, freedom from high-speed traffic and open space. Since only 15 per cent of the ground area is built over, there is plenty of space for garages, gardens, parks, nurseries, playing fields and swimming pools. Even the roofs of the building are used for recreation, and the housing area as a whole is surrounded by a wide green belt, separating it from the factories, giving a city zoned into four main areas—housing, factories, culture and administration.

Le Corbusier developed these ideas in a series of projects both for actual cities and the ideal. The plan Voisin of 1925 shows 'the city of three million' applied to a huge area of Paris, with giant skyscrapers, motorways and a super population density of around 13,000 people per acre. In the plans for Algiers, the housing strip is developed into a linear city with the motorway on top of the building. But the clearest statement of his ideas is in *The Radiant City (La Ville Radieuse)*, compiled in response to a questionnaire from city officials in Russia asking for suggestions on the replanning of Moscow. Like many technocrats, Le Corbusier claimed that his work was above politics, merely the logical rational outcome of the modern world.

In this world, production was in factories, and it was mass-production. The factories were operated by a proletariat who required standardized mass housing and they were administered by an intellectual élite who required an administrative centre. The working day was to be reduced—another advantage of mass-production—to five hours per day, so cultural and leisure facilities would be needed. Finally a transportation system was needed to link up, like a nerve system, the various parts of the body industrial. As long as these are the ingredients, and politics is just a matter of who holds authority, then it is true that 'plans are not politics' and the solutions of technocrats are independent of the ambitions of politicians.

Thus *The Radiant City* is dedicated to 'Authority', and it did not particularly matter to Le Corbusier whether it was the authority of party bureaucrats or the authority of industrialists and bankers, though he used to claim that 'town planning is a way of making money'. What mattered was that the authority was strong enough to carry out the plan—he greatly admired Napoleon III under whose organization Haussmann had transformed Paris. For the 'plan' was all important:

> The plan is dictator! Let each specialist establish the plans which are in conformity with the new times . . . once these plans are made, discussion is closed, doubt swept away, certainty assured. . . . Plans are the rational and poetic monument set up in the midst of contingencies. Contingencies are the environment: places, peoples, cultures, topographies, climates. They are furthermore, the resources liberated by modern techniques. The latter are universal.

The plan of the Radiant City, as the direct consequence of these 'universal modern techniques', is the urban equivalent of factory production. In the factory the stages of manufacture are separated out and rationalized, so in the city the activities of life are separated into discrete parts. In turn, the parts are standardized—administration into skyscrapers and housing into slabs—because standardization too was seen as a characteristic and beneficial result of mass-production. Through it, the city would be a place

Top: Paolo Soleri, the creator of Arcology, shown here working with students
Above: Arcosanti is being built by Soleri and his followers in the Arizona desert

of order, with 'a universal standard and complete uniformity in detail. Under such conditions the mind is calm.' The Radiant City represents the division of labour on a metropolitan scale, as a city planning technique, with the transportation system in the position of the assembly line, that brings all the fragmented 'parts' together as a final product.

However it has become a truism that the division of labour, for all its 'efficiency', not only divides the work, but also divides the worker who has to live with it. Similarly the Radiant City divides the life of the city dweller into standardized parts, with housing in one place, work in another and leisure somewhere else. It has proved more difficult to draw together a fragmented life than it is to assemble an industrial product. Thus the subsequent success of the Radiant City as a model for city planning has meant that the alienation of industrial capitalism has been reproduced, literally, in the physical arrangements of our environment. This model of

Below: Soleri has produced many designs for Arcologies. The Arcologies, of which Hexahedron is one, are huge concentrated cities

the ideal city, which had become orthodox by the end of the World War II, was based on the myth that industrial mass-production could be applied to everything, and that this would lead to untold benefits for all. During the 1950s and 1960s a similar myth about the benefits to be gained from automation led to an image of the ideal city based, not on production, but on consumption.

Towards a Brave New Architecture

'Progress', wrote Oscar Wilde, 'is the realization of utopias', and the period since the World War II has seen an official devotion to the idea of progress that would have warmed the heart of Francis Bacon. So much so, that the realization of many of the promises of science and technology has led people to doubt whether that sort of progress (or that sort of utopia) is necessarily a good idea. However, just as the utopias of the past have been pursued in the name of progress, so new utopias and ideal cities have been created, and at times it has looked as if people have been using Huxley's *Brave New World* as a utopian text book, rather than a cautionary tale.

A new cult of the ideal city flared up and subsided during the 1960s, under the influence of such disparate phenomena as computers, transistors, space probes, automation, miniaturization. Psychedelic drugs, swinging London and San Francisco and the unbounded, if unfounded, optimism that tends to grip people in times of economic plenty were the visible signs. Again the justification was that the contemporary form of settlement was out of tune with a new situation, that a scientific and technological revolution demanded a new outlook, and that an artificial urbanized future was necessary, beneficial and inevitable. In addition, technological change was now so rapid, and had such a momentum of its own, that, left to themselves, the social developments could no longer keep pace.

The answer lay in 'total planning' and a 'new vision'—in short, a new technological utopia, in which scientist and inventor were to be joined by the 'designer'. Where Le Corbusier and others had split the city into separate bits, the designers of 'megastructures' tried to draw everything back together, if not into a single building then into a single system or image. The results were so big that they dwarfed the not inconsiderable renewal schemes of contemporary planners as a dinosaur might dwarf a lizard. But as a species they proved far less successful than the dinosaur. By the time megastructures were collected, explained and justified by Justus Dalinden in 1971 in his book *Urban Structures of the Future,* they were rapidly nearing extinction, with the notable exception of American-based architect Paolo Soleri's arcologies.

Arcologies, with names such as babel-canyon, asteromo, 3d jersey, arcube, novanoah −1 and hexahedron, were human habitations designed according to the principles of Arcology, or Ecological Architecture: 'in arcology the city is conceived as a three-dimensional entity, architecture becomes ecological due to the magnitude of scale and complexity'. Soleri was distressed that the urban population of the world had spread out, under the influence of the motor car, into 'a weak veneer of life ridden with blight and stillness', and felt that the general lack of spiritual and moral cohesiveness (order) could be attributed to this dispersal. In place of urban sprawl and suburbia, Arcology would compress all human life into huge structures containing hundreds of thousands of people per square mile. 'Arcology, instrumented by science and technology, will be an aestheto-compassionate phenomenon. Its advent will be the implosion of the flat megalopolis of today into an urban solid of superdense and human vitality.'

At a stroke, most of the environmental and spiritual problems besetting mankind would be solved.

> Aggression and guilt are in good proportion a bridge of a sort connecting meaninglessness to meaningfulness. Therefore a better bridge must be found. If man is really in need of risk and violence, if frustration and guilt are really tearing society asunder, then the awesomeness of arcology and the com-

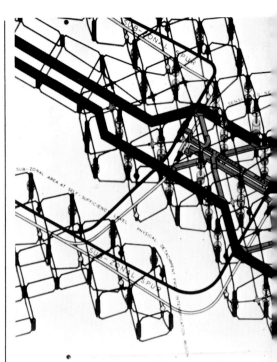

Above: Plug-in City presented consumer choice as the most perfect expression of personal freedom. The drawing shows the complex servicing network for this consumption

plexity of its construction are positive alternatives to war, social strife and squalor.

Similarly Arcology could solve problems of waste, shortage of natural resources, domination of industry by motor manufacturers, loss of scale in the environment, planned obsolescence, leisure, segregation, old age, politics and so on, including the problems of underdeveloped countries— the 'paupers' of the world economy.

Arcology is in the form of huge symmetrical structures that are intended to present, on the outside, a coherent, contained image, with no anarchic ragged edges, at the same time as allowing the maximum personal variety within. People should have individual freedom, while still feeling that they are part of some meaningful whole. However, it often reads very much like a conventional town plan, except that people in an Arcology could walk anywhere in just a few minutes. They also had immediate access to the countryside, for Arcologies took up so little land compared to contemporary cities that more land was available for cultivation and leisure. They gave all the benefits of town and country, not rolled into one, but existing side by side as polar opposites.

The immense functional advantages aside, it was their spiritual and biological aspects that made arcologies such a godsend to mankind, especially in the way they achieve miniaturization, 'one of the fundamental rules of evolution'.

> Now that the inquietude of man is turned to the construction of the superorganism, which society is, a new phase of miniaturiza-tion is imperative. Arcology is a step towards it. Arcological miniaturization will cause the scale of the world to 'expand', and will also make feasible the migration of man to the seas and orbital lands.

Obviously, this would lead, in an arcology of say, a thousand people, to the 'miniaturizing implosion of the social body' accompanied by a 'micro-explosion of the thousands towards the periphery of miniaturized organism'. Thus arcologies were not just ingenious sculptural boxes into which people were crammed tightly so that there was no room for them to bring their problems in with them, they were a new kind of superorganism in which computers and other cybernetic devices tied together the brains of the citizens into a higher consciousness. Arcologies were to be biological organisms themselves, as well as containers for biological life.

Most utopians have had difficulty with finance, and Soleri has been no different; as he willingly admitted, arcologies would be expensive. He has designed over 30 arcologies with extensive and detailed models and drawings of them all. In 1970, the Cosanti Foundation, a non-profit-making body set up in Arizona to test Soleri's ideas by experiment, bought land to begin work on the thirtieth arcology—Arcosanti. They meant to test, with a population of 3,000, whether people can really live in the close proximity envisaged by arcology. The successful utopian experiments of the nineteenth century were those that possessed a strong to dictatorial leadership, demanded absolute religious faith, and engaged in a heavy building programme. Arcosanti would appear to have all three in abundance.

Soleri continues to work on the same themes that preoccupied him during the 1960s, and he still attracts sufficient disciples and funds to keep the Cosanti Foundation in existence. His ideas have achieved greater longevity than those of almost all the other megastructure designers, for, while Soleri embraces high technology, he also *opposes* many aspects of a mass-production industry and economy. He does not rate mobility as a 'good thing' in itself, prophesies the extinction of the motor car, attacks waste and built-in obsolescence, and uses the word ecology. He puts forward an ideal of human life that makes use of high technology, but does not consume technological 'goodies' in the manner of an affluent society. Somewhere, amongst the gobbledegook, there's an idea of 'higher things'.

The Affluent City

For some of the other 'dinosaurs' however, consumer society itself seemed to represent the apogee of human achievement, and the exercise of consumer choice was the most perfect expression of personal freedom. In both Plug-In City by the English design group Archigram, and the Spatial City by the French architect Yona Friedman, this area of liberty was extended from the refrigerator and other household commodities to the dwelling itself.

The 'megastructure' of Plug-In City consisted of a diagonal framework of structural tubes containing the necessary city services, such as electricity, water, and sewage, including passenger lifts and the distribution of goods. It had a projected life of 40 years. Everything else—dwellings, offices, shops, theatres, car parks, exhibition halls, monorails, escalators—were plugged into or draped over the megastructure. They were lifted into place by cranes permanently positioned at high points in the megastructure, so that units could be easily replaced when they became obsolete. Plug-In units were mass-produced in factories, exactly like motor cars, with choice of colours, styling, standard extras, new models each year and, of course, built-in obsolescence.

Plug-In City represented the consummation, as it were, of architecture's long flirtation with the motor industry, an affair that went back at least as far as the Futurists. Even Archigram's general prescription for the future read like the advertising copy for a new model—'The future must be comfortable . . . reassurance, lack of tension, peace of mind as well as peace of posture . . . personalized . . . responsive . . . smoother, less demonstrative . . . the future will offer "features", value for money, optional extras. . .'

Plug-In City offered many opportunities for buying and selling, and for leisure, but took little account of production. Although it had offices, laboratories and business centres, it was never clear where the various plugs were manufactured, or by whom. They were perhaps immaculate conceptions of the megastructure. Whereas Plug-In City was essentially Consumer City, the 'leisure' and the 'play' themes of the affluent society were developed by Yona Friedman in his Spatial City. Its megastructure was to be a rectilinear frame, raised *above* an existing city, leaving it 'undisturbed'.

Like Plug-In City, it would be possible to put anything anywhere, and to move it about at will. Friedman saw leisure and 'play' as essential parts of life, and thus mobility and change were not just conveniences or something one had to put up with, but basic biological needs. Clearly if everyone 'needed' these things then it was only 'democratic' that everyone should have them. People could therefore 'choose' their home by computer, change its plan and equipment, and move it about. All of this, of course, meant that people had more 'freedom', and democracy was extended from the choosing of one's parliamentary representative to choosing the location of one's home through the impersonal ballot-box of the computer.

The high status of change and mobility fed on the belief that the discoveries of science and the high spots of technology, such as space probes, must eventually become generalized and transform the daily life of everyone. The technological and industrial factors in human society and settlements were given greater and greater importance, until it was proposed to arrange daily life for the efficiency of the technology, rather than to have the technology at the service of life. From this arises the linear city concept where settlement has been brought to the means of transport, and not the other way round, with the eventual development that the city itself should move—as seen in the many projects for floating cities and Archigram's famous walking city.

The New Status of Nature

When the ideal city itself became mobile, it meant that the city had become self-contained and independent of the ground, that is, it had drastically changed its relationship with nature. Most utopians have paid attention

144

Previous page: General view over Plug-in City, with mobile office blocks. All accommodation is designed for regular replacement and 'plugs' into the slightly more permanent 'megastructure'

to the soil, whether it was the Renaissance ideal city controlling the necessary land for survival, or the citizens of Thomas More's Amaurote taking turns at agricultural labour—they stress the importance of working with nature. But the development of industry has led to a greater and greater antagonism between 'civilization' and 'nature', between town and country. Industry proved to be such a prodigious source of riches that utopias were invented in which people survive independently of nature—from industrial production alone. In Aldous Huxley's *Brave New World,* for instance, even the production of human life was moved into the factory, and 'artificial' materials were prized above all others.

In the ideal city this trend was illustrated by the complete separation of the city from the ground, and in the idea that settlements could be concentrated, say under a dome, leaving 'nature' to return to the wild. Thus the country stopped being the place where people work in co-operation with nature, and became a 'natural' wilderness whose wild and untouched qualities set off the 'civilization' of the city. Meanwhile food was made in the factory, synthesized from fossil fuels with the help of nuclear power. For, of course, the 'nature' in the above antagonism was seen as the fertile surface of the earth with its trees, fields and lakes. Mineral resources, particularly fossil and nuclear fuels were rarely considered as 'nature'. When the food was moved to the factory, then utopia did not become liberated or free from nature, but merely exchanged dependence on renewable resources for dependence on non-renewable resources. Similarly the supposed 'freedom' achieved in Plug-In City and Spatial City by liberating the dwelling from a fixed plot of land is just the freedom to be dependent on the 'megastructure'.

Spaceship Earth

It is ironical that a person who contributed so much to the cult of high technology should also have been instrumental in proposing the conservation of natural resources. However, Buckminster Fuller has managed both and in doing so, invented one of the most potent images of modern 'alternative' utopia, the geodesic dome.

Fuller designed several ideal cities of the megastructure class, but he also developed the concept of 'Spaceship Earth' in which the world is seen as a limited entity, with limited energy income from the sun, and limited 'reserves' in the energy bank. Thus he stresses that resources should be used with greater and greater efficiency, as in the case of, say, 'a one-tenth ton Telstar satellite outperforming 75,000 tons of transatlantic cable'. Utopia would be possible only if technology provided more and more goods from fewer and fewer resources.

> [It] was impossible when people thought that there was only enough for a minority to live in comfort. But utopia is, inherently, for all or for none. Because invisible technology can do much less, utopia is now possible for the first time. Bodily needs must precede metaphysical contentment.

During the 1960s Fuller inaugurated the World Design Science Decade to stimulate the achievement of this utopia, for he believed that the state of society was such that a utopia was necessary to ensure its survival:

> Let us . . . commit ourselves earnestly to the Design Science Decade approach to achieving utopia. This moment of realization that it soon must be utopia or oblivion coincides exactly with the discovery by man that, for the first time in history, utopia is, at least, physically possible of human attainment.

Most of the people discussed in this section believed that science and technology were far more important to utopia than mere social or political matters. Buckminster Fuller is emphatic in adding *design* to the list. 'There is only one revolution tolerable to all men, all societies and all systems', he wrote, 'Revolution by Design and Invention'. However, it should not

be surprising to find the designer occupying a role as utopian, for design is the necessary link between scientific theory and a usable product. Moreover, a designer's work inevitably involves speculations and assumptions about the future, however much that might be clothed in professional jargon. Indeed, if progress is the realization of utopias, it is to a considerable extent designers who turn the technical utopias into working projects and programmes.

The utopian assumptions of these projects need close scrutiny and it should not be assumed that they are for the good of all. For knowledge, scientific or otherwise, may be a wonderful thing, but its use in utopia is rarely disinterested or beneficial to all, as is well illustrated by the control and manipulation of knowledge in Plato's republic. Just as in Plato's time, competing concepts of utopia co-exist—the utopia of the stable state with the utopia of freedom and co-operation. To date, science and design have almost exclusively served the former, but, if it is, as Fuller claims, a matter of utopia or oblivion, then it might be appropriate for science to change sides.

Above: Buckminster Fuller is concerned with the potential of geodesic structures and high technology. Here New York is rescued by the device of a vast air-conditioned dome

Utopia or Oblivion?

When Edward Bellamy drafted his plan for an ideal society in 1888, he built it on a system of economic and labour relationships, on an industrial army of labour. Aspects of life, such as morals or marriage, that classical utopians like More or Plato took care to regulate through the state, were left by Bellamy to the tender mercies of reason and public opinion. In making economics the central preoccupation of his state, he was merely reproducing the opinion of his era, that economic relationships, internal and international, were the key to the well-being of all.

Utopian writers, partly inspired by massive advances in communications, soon felt the necessity to propose ideal solutions on a global scale. Where More was content with one ideal state that resolved its problems with its neighbours by violence and conquest, Bellamy sees international disputes resolved by ideal economic relationships, and H. G. Wells would turn utopia itself into a world state.

The World State

A Modern Utopia, which was published by Wells in 1905 at the height of the imperial era, is not so much a prescription for utopia as an extensive discourse on the utopias of the past and the possibilities of the present. It is notable for its legal and administrative complexity and its pursuit of efficiency through centralization. Regulations cover all aspects of life, though not to the point of coercion; nevertheless idiots, criminals, drunkards and other such deviants would be exiled to obscure islands, but with separate places of exile for men and women so that their vices would not

Left: Self-determination, democracy and self-sufficiency are perennial utopian ambitions. Here they are claimed and expressed in a Chinese rural commune

be reproduced. A vast index system keeps detailed records of the life of every person on the planet, private property and inheritance are limited but not removed, and all production is regulated by the state so that unemployment no longer exists. The rule of the World State is in the hands of a volunteer élite called the Samurai, who must be highly educated and lead a spartan life according to a prescribed rule.

Wells associates science, centralization and industry with human progress and he retains these in his other utopia, *Men like Gods,* in which he takes a less jaundiced view of human nature and drops all the business of a world state in favour of universal education. The pursuit of this sort of progress in the real world has meant that there have been very few traditional utopias in this century. However, their place has been more than filled by official dreams such as the New Deal, the Soviet 'five-year plans', the long-term strategies of the international corporations, and in such steps towards world government as the League of Nations.

Instead it has been a century of anti-utopia. In Aldous Huxley's *Brave New World,* the pursuit of progress and stability has led to a totally manufactured society where the inhabitants themselves are mass-produced and conditioned to fit every level and role of the industrial structure. Industrial society has been taken to a point where happiness and satisfaction are merely chemically induced 'feelings', and concepts such as liberty, justice or self-determination have become irrelevant. Productivity and progress have become ends in themselves, and humanity must serve them.

Beyond Freedom and Dignity

Futures based on the potentialities of combining science with the state reach their most horrific realization in George Orwell's *1984.* Alongside Huxley's satire, it formed part of the cultural climate of the 1950s and 1960s and a whole generation was brought up on the imagery of these two powerful anti-utopias. The possible police state of *1984* fully exploits the resources for scientific surveillance and information storage, and, just as Huxley's work has proved prophetic, we now have the technology for Orwell's authoritarian corporate state.

It can be seen in the ubiquitous computer credit records, and in the surveillance and computer systems of places such as Northern Ireland where personal records exist on over half the population and the situation provides a testing ground for devices intended to protect the state, whatever its political 'colour'. In *1984,* every room is equipped with a two-way television by means of which the police may tune in to any conversation anywhere. Not only do individuals disappear, but by control of the recording systems, newspapers, registries and official histories, it can be demonstrated that they never existed. Behind the parody, Soviet Russia of the 1930s stands out clearly and the similarities of method are sometimes uncanny.

A year before Orwell published his anti-utopia in 1949, Bernard Skinner published *Walden Two,* a real utopia, but one in which the conditioned society comes into its own. He shows a community which lives in harmony through the deep and systematic conditioning of its members, not by aversion, but by positive reinforcement towards the 'feelings' of happiness. 'Our members are practically always doing what they want to do,' he claims, 'what they "choose" to do—but we see to it that they will want to do precisely the things which are best for themselves and the community. Their behaviour is determined, yet they're free.' Orwell's world was in a constant state of war and the methods used for control were in the main external, but Skinner's world is one where societal controls have gone inside. If a person is nothing more than a product of society, he asks, why don't we use this positively to create a better race? Where Orwell's novel revolves around an inner-directed individual who kicks against the system, Skinner revels in the ability to remove this kind of asocial individual by conditioning.

Where Huxley satirized the consequences of centralization, mechanization and the industrial economy and showed how values and concepts such as freedom, dignity and justice would be destroyed, Skinner sees

Above: Many of the preoccupations of utopia as the ideal state were brought up to date in Orwell's anti-utopia, 1984, with its repressive morality, psychological manipulation and a class of near-slaves Right: Bibliography for three ways of life today, by Paul and Percival Goodman: I Efficient Consumption; II Elimination of the difference between production and consumption; III Planned security with minimum regulation

these concepts themselves as the cause of society's problems. The aim, then, is not to find a perfect society where freedom, dignity and justice reign, but to abolish all vestiges of such unnecessary pre-scientific concepts. The result is, not a society of freedom, but one which does not have the word in its vocabulary.

Orwell's *1984* could be described as the anti-utopia of order and control, whereas Skinner's *Walden Two,* is the utopia of order and control. But the immediate post-war years also saw an attempt to resurrect the libertarian utopias of the nineteenth century, bringing them up to date and incorporating the developments of the intervening 50 years.

Communitas

Communitas, by the two young Americans Paul and Percival Goodman, one a poet and writer and the other an architect, was described at the time of publication in 1947 as a badly needed revival in utopian thinking. They argue that there is a direct relationship between the way a society organizes the design and layout of its cities and rural areas, and the dominant values of the society. Thus they explore utopia by showing the way that town planning organizes the processes of production and consumption. As we have seen, the idea that the physical arrangement of a country express its values is common in utopian schemes, and many of their creators from Campanella to Owen gave the ideal society an ideal symbolic form. The Goodmans studied past societies and what they offered, and they themselves offered three alternatives for a planned future, based on three different sets of social values: Efficient Consumption (based on abundances); the Elimination of the Difference between Consumption and Production; and Planned Security with Minimum Regulation.

By offering three alternatives they make their own values and objectives clearer, and the utopia they desire is Future Two. In a revised edition of 1960 they show that Future One had been embraced by society and they

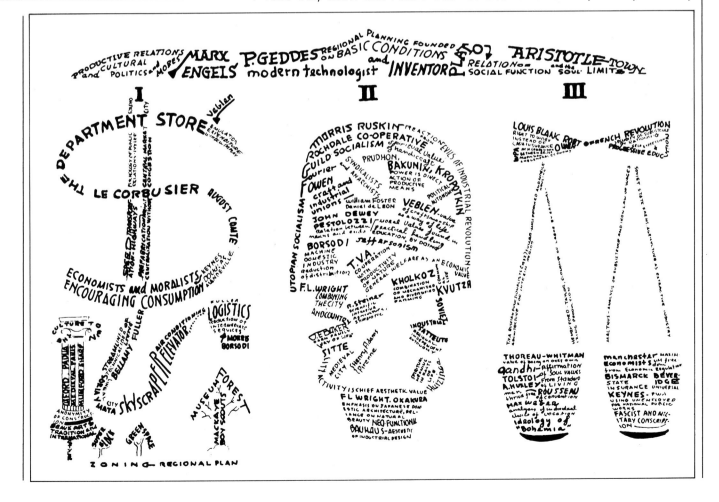

PHILIP CASTLE

Two conflicting dreams.
Left: The official utopia of consumption, as projected in an advertizing handout for a new city being built in England at Milton Keynes
Above: Drop City in the Rockies, built on the dream of freedom from urban consumption, with dome dwellings made from the material waste of consumer society

related it to the New York City of that year: 'our cultural climate and the state of ideas are such that our surplus, of means and wealth, leads only to extravagant repetitions of the air-conditioned nightmare . . . a pattern of life that used to be unsatisfactory, and now, by extravagance, becomes absurd'. However, they point out that production depends on consumption; modern metropolitan society, though capable of great productivity, fails in the necessary 'consumption attitudes'. Future One rectifies this by analysing 'how men can be as efficiently wasteful as possible'.

Future Two is designed to achieve a close relationship between home and work by organizing production in small workshops or in the home. Each worker is involved in deciding what to produce, the design of the product and the actual production process, so everyone has a diversified career doing different jobs. All this would take place in relatively self-sufficient small units which integrate farm and factory, and no one would live more than a cycle-ride from their daily occupation. All members of the community, young and old, would find varied and satisfying productive work, with factory workers helping in the fields during peak periods, and farmers reciprocating in the workshops during the slack.

Children too would be involved so that work becomes a natural part of their lives, and they would be encouraged to learn and explore for themselves and to create independent lives of their own. After the age of dependence, the Goodmans suggest, they might live in a house with other children rather than in the home of their parents. Their aim is to integrate work and life, to maximize creative work, to make every part of life valuable in itself, and, like Morris, to turn both life and work into art.

The Age of Instant Plenty

However, it was not to be expected that *Communitas* should stand in the way of 'progress', and the next 20 years saw a strenuous and singleminded pursuit of Future One in our society. All problems were to evaporate in the face of high consumption and abundance, brought about by technologically induced economic growth. Just as Fourier had placed the Age of Harmony at the end of 32 stages of history, and Winstanley had described the rule of Reason in terms of the Third Age, so the industrial ideal was explained by W. W. Rostow as the culmination of four stages of industrial development.

His theory was intended to offer an alternative to Marxism which maintained that a revolution was necessary before everyone would gain the benefits of technology. According to Rostow, industrial evolution was inevitably leading to the goal of plenty for all, so why bother with the revolution? It was an age of consensus in which ideology was dead. The problem of the capitalist trade cycle was now solved, and there was nothing left but a steady climb towards abundance. Even peace was assured now that the technology of the bomb had created an inevitable state of suspended aggression. Bureaucrats and politicians could sleep peacefully in their beds and the English prime minister Macmillan was right, when he claimed: 'You've never had it so good'.

Of course, there were non-believers, like campaigners for nuclear disarmament or equally crazy revolutionists, but they would be overtaken by the inevitable climax of prosperity. Science and technology had become the religion of post-war society, and all it needed was a priesthood in the form of a technological meritocracy to lead us to the promised land. Where many previous societies had been fascinated by the eternal and unchanging aspects of life, we were preoccupied with change. Technology was revolutionizing the whole way of life. And, as the Bible said, it was good.

Appropriately enough, the utopias that were popular at this time, like *Brave New World* and *Walden Two,* were those where science and technology transcended morals. *1984* meanwhile showed the folly of pursuing an ideology, and effectively put utopian speculation out of court. The answer lay to hand: the world was a stage upon which all mankind was to reach the technological millennium, and nature was a bountiful backdrop providing resources for all, as well as the cardboard cut-out for the rustic image.

The Springs of Hope

At the height of the era of mass consumption, astonishingly, cracks began to appear. In 1962 Rachel Carson showed, in *Silent Spring,* that nature was not a toy backdrop that sprang back into place after technology had finished with it. It lay down and died. In the same year Aldous Huxley published his true utopia *Island,* where Buddhism, sexual yoga, mind-expanding drugs, western and traditional medicine and advanced plant breeding and agriculture all combine in a sane, joyful, unaggressive, achieving society. But Pala, the island, has oil, and the novel ends with murder, invasion, and a coup to pave the way for western oil interests.

The search for a new politics and direction is reflected in the events of 1968 in the USA, Britain, Czechoslovakia and France. Faith in industry and the state, in the society of abundance and consumption, had been shaken, and it was never to be quite the same again. In Britain the peace movement and CND gave rise to a little journal called *Resurgence,* which called for 'a steadier tempo of social progress together with a more dispersed structure of power'. It emphasized that above a certain size all power becomes oligarchical and that we should move to a much smaller scale of organization which could be controlled by everyone. Small was not inefficient, as claimed by the sages of industrialism, but it was beautiful.

At the end of the 1960s, the growing awareness of 'ecology' finally hit the headlines, and by mid-1970 almost everyone in the industralized world had heard of it. It slipped slowly from view as the news media moved on to greener pastures, but not before it had been added to the increasingly critical analysis of industrial society. Paris had renewed the dream of a world as different from corporate state capitalism as it was from state socialism. The ecological crisis showed that society's unrestrained exploitation of nature to create an age of abundance was destroying our long-term existence on the planet. The result has been a rebirth of the utopia of the decentralized community, but developed to take good social and self-sufficient advantage of the scientific advances of the last 20 years.

It has shown itself in an enormous proliferation of communes and communities where people are trying to live without exploiting nature and without exploiting each other. They have taken inspiration from a very wide range of religious, social, and political beliefs, but all share a rejection of the values and prescribed way of life of industrial society. However, the utopian upsurge of today is not just another turn in a never-ending cycle of hope and despair, but a necessary alternative in a world that could easily be killing itself. Ideas that were once branded as utopian, unrealistic, unhistorical and impractical have now become a key to survival.

Hand-in-hand with the theory and practice of decentralization has gone the development of a technology on which such a society could be based, so-called 'radical' or 'alternative' technology. Although for many of its creators it is part and parcel of a radically altered social structure, it may have the potential to be used to sustain the existing structure. By 1973, international capitalism had added the oil crisis to its problems, and alternative technology has become a major concern of supporters of the 'business as usual' perspective as well as the supporters of the decentralized utopia. The alternatives to fossil fuels—solar, wind and wave power—were serious propositions. Whether alternative technology will get the developed industrial nations off the hook, or will lead to a new libertarian age, remains to be seen.

The dream of a decentralized society can look to a long tradition that goes back through the Goodmans, Kropotkin and Morris to Winstanley, John Ball, Zeno and even to the dreams of an earthly paradise. Similarly the advocates of the centralized state boast a parallel tradition through Bellamy and Saint-Simon, to Bacon, Campanella and Plato. But today's dream of the earthly paradise derives, not from an analysis of historical precedent, but, as with many earlier dreams, from a reaction in the hearts and minds of people who have lived through the era of supposed mass-consumption and the mess it creates. So far its literature has been in the form of analytical articles and books and its practice in the form of relatively isolated experiments and communities.

Below: If all the injustices of the world were removed tomorrow, William Morris asked, what else would people be obliged, by necessity, to do but their daily work? Utopia, for all its freedom and leisure, can only be based on varied, non-polluting, democratically controlled and enjoyable daily work

154

Before long someone will put together an updated version of *News from Nowhere* as an inspiration to change on a wider scale. Such a transformation faces political problems as great as those that faced their predecessors. As it was for Winstanley, the central question is one of popular control and access to natural resources, and particularly to the land.

> Take notice that England is not a free people till the poor that have no land have a free allowance to dig and labour the commons, and so live as comfortably as the landlords that live in their enclosures. For the people have not laid out their monies and shed their blood that their landlords, the Norman power, should still have its liberty and freedom to rule in tyranny . . . but that the oppressed might be set free, prison doors opened, and the people's hearts comforted by a universal consent of making the earth a common treasury, that they may live together . . . united in brotherly love into one spirit; and having a comfortable livelihood in the community of one earth their mother.

Bibliography

GENERAL BOOKS
publication dates are of latest editions

BAUMAN, Z. *Socialism: The Active Utopia* (Allen & Unwin, London 1976; Holmes & Meier, New York 1976)

BERNERI, M. *Journey through Utopia* (Schocken Books, New York 1971)

BERNSTEIN, E. *Cromwell and Communism* (Frank Cass, London 1963; Schocken Books, New York 1963)

CONRADS, U. & SPERLICH, H. *Fantastic Architecture* (Architectural Press, London 1963)

DAHINDEN, J. *Urban Structures for the Future* (Pall Mall Press, London 1972)

EVENSON, N. *Le Corbusier: The Machine and the Grand Design* (Studio Vista, London 1969; Braziller, New York 1969)

HAYDEN, D. *Seven American Utopias* (MIT Press, Cambridge, Mass., 1976)

HERTZLER, J. *The History of Utopian Thought* (Macmillan, New York 1923)

HILL, C. *The World Turned Upside Down* (Penguin Books, Harmondsworth 1975)

HILL, C. & DELL, E. *The Good Old Cause: The English Revolution of 1640–60* (Frank Cass, London 1969)

HINE, R. V. *California's Utopian Colonies* (Yale University Press, New Haven, Connecticut 1966)

KATEB, G. *Utopia and Its Enemies* (Schocken Books, New York 1972)

KOPP, A. *Town and Revolution* (Thames & Hudson, London 1970; Braziller, New York 1970)

MORTON, A. L. *The English Utopia* (Lawrence & Wishart, London 1969)

MORTON, A. L. *The Story of Utopias* (Lawrence & Wishart, London 1941; Viking Press, New York 1962)

MORTON, A. L. *The World of the Ranters* (Lawrence & Wishart, London 1970)

PEHNT, W. *Expressionist Architecture* (Thames & Hudson, London 1973; Praeger, New York 1974)

RASMUSSEN, S. E. *Towns and Buildings* (MIT Press, Cambridge, Mass., 1969)

RAWSON, E. *The Spartan Tradition in European Thought* (Oxford University Press, Oxford 1969)

ROSENAU, H. *Social Purpose in Architecture* (Studio Vista, London 1970)

ROSENAU, H. *Boullée and Visionary Architecture* (Academy Editions, London 1976; Harmony Books, New York 1976)

RUDKIN, O. D. *Thomas Spence and His Connections* (Kelley, Clifton, NJ, 1970)

THOMPSON, E. P. *The Making of the English Working Class* (Penguin Books, Harmondsworth 1970)

THOMPSON, E. P. *William Morris: Romantic to Revolutionary* (Merlin Press, London 1977; Pantheon, New York 1977)

WATERS, A. W. *The Trial of Thomas Spence* (Courier Press, Leamington Spa 1917)

SELECTED UTOPIAN TEXTS

ALBERTI, L. B. *The Complete Works* trans. F. Borsi (Harper & Row, New York 1976)

ANDREAE, J. V. *Christianopolis* trans. F. Enilheld (Oxford University Press, Oxford 1916)

AUGUSTINE, St. *The City of God* ed. D. Knowles (Penguin Books, Harmondsworth 1972)

BACON, F. *The Advancement of Learning and New Atlantis* (Oxford University Press, Oxford 1938)

BELLAMY, E. *Looking Backward* (Harvard University Press, Cambridge, Mass., 1967)

BURKE, E. *Reflections on the Revolution in France* ed. Conor Cruise O'Brien (Penguin Books, Harmondsworth 1969)

CABET, E. *Voyage en Icarie* 1848 edition reprinted (Kelley, Clifton, NJ, 1971)

COBBETT, W. *Rural Rides* ed. George Woodcock (Penguin Books, Harmondsworth 1967)

CORBUSIER, LE *The Complete Architectural Works* ed. W. Boesiger (Artemis Verlag, Zürich 1966; Thames & Hudson, London 1966; Wittenborn, New York 1966)

DE FOIGNEY, G. *Les Aventures de Jacques Sadeur dans La Découverte et Le Voyage de La Terre Australe* 1692 edition reprinted (Clearwater Publishing, New York 1974)

ENGELS, F. *The Condition of the Working Class in England* (Lawrence & Wishart, London 1973)

ENGELS, F. *Socialism, Utopian and Scientific* (Pathfinder Press, New York 1972)

FULLER, R. BUCKMINSTER *Buckminster Fuller Reader* ed. James Meller (Penguin Books, Harmondsworth 1972)

GODWIN, W. *An Enquiry Concerning Political Justice* ed. Isaac Kramnick (Penguin Books, Harmondsworth 1976)

GOODMAN, PAUL & PERCIVAL *Communitas* (Vintage Books, New York 1973)

HOBBES, T. *Leviathan* ed. C. B. Macpherson (Penguin Books, Harmondsworth 1968)

HOWARD, E. *Garden Cities of Tomorrow* (Faber & Faber, London 1945)

HUXLEY, A. *Brave New World* (Penguin Books, Harmondsworth 1969)

HUXLEY, A. *Island* (Panther Books, St. Albans 1977; Harper & Row, New York 1962)

KROPOTKIN, P. *Fields, Factories and Workshops Tomorrow* ed. C. Ward (Allen & Unwin, London 1974; Harper & Row, New York 1974)

MARX, K. *Selected Writings in Sociology and Social Philosophy* eds. T. B. Bottomore & M. Rubel (Penguin Books, Harmondsworth 1970)

MARX, K. & ENGELS, F. *Collected Works* (International Publishers, New York 1975)

MORRIS, W. *Three Works* ed. A. L. Morton (Lawrence & Wishart, London 1974; International Publishers, New York 1974)

MORRIS, W. *Political Writings* ed. A. L. Morton (Lawrence & Wishart, London 1973; International Publishers, New York 1973)

ORWELL, G. *Nineteen Eighty-Four* (Penguin Books, Harmondsworth 1970)

PLATO *The Republic* ed. M. Cornford (Oxford University Press, New York 1970)

PLUTARCH *The Rise and Fall of Athens* trans. I. Scott-Kilvert (Penguin Books, Harmondsworth 1970)

PROUDHON, P-J *Selected Writings* ed. S. Edwards (Macmillan, London 1970)

SANDERS, N. K. *The Epic of Gilgamesh* (Penguin Books, Harmondsworth 1970)

SKINNER, B. F. *Walden Two* (Collier-Macmillan, London 1962)

TAUT, B. *Alpine Architecture* trans. S. Palmer (November Books, London 1972)

WELLS, H. G. *A Modern Utopia* (University of Nebraska Press, Nebraska 1967)

WHITE, F. R. *Famous Utopias of the Renaissance* (Hendricks House, New York 1955)

WIEBENSON, D. *Tony Garnier: The Cité Industrielle* (Braziller, New York 1969)

WINSTANLEY, G. *The Law of Freedom and Other Writings* ed. C. Hill (Penguin Books, Harmondsworth 1973)

WRIGHT, F. L. *Writings and Buildings* (Horizon Press, New York 1976)

Index

Acknowledgments

This book would have been impossible without the many friends with whom the ideas, people and issues that it raises have been discussed over and over again. In particular the authors would like to thank Judy Etheridge, Ingrid Kolmschlag, Howard Liddell and Alison Ravetz. In addition we should like to thank the students and staff at Hull School of Architecture who have contributed in many ways, not least by their tolerance. Special thanks are due to Sandra, Veronica, Norman and Steph for their help in typing from what was at times an illegible manuscript.

Nobody but ourselves is responsible for the omissions, inaccuracies and downright mistakes, some of which are inevitable in so personal a selection from the incredible range of utopian material. Finally we would like to thank the utopians themselves whose ideas and exploits have been such a vast source of stimulation and enjoyment to us.

We are grateful to the following for permission to reproduce photographs on pages:
8–9 Lehman Collection/Bulloz; 10 Louvre/Giraudon; 11 Monaco Pinacoteca/IGDA; 12 British Library; 13 Memling Museum, Bruges/Scala; 14 Lucca Biblioteca Statale/Scala; 15 Victoria and Albert Museum; 16 Schwitter Library; 17 Florence Convents. Marco/Pucciarelli; 18 Museo Nazionale/Scala; 20 Radio Times Hulton Picture Library; 20 (bottom) National Gallery, London; 21 (bottom) Bulloz; 22–23 Scala; 24 Mansell Collection; 25 (top) Mary Evans Picture Library; 25 (bottom) Radio Times Hulton Picture Library; 26 Vatican Rome/IGDA; 28 Giraudon; 29 Radio Times Hulton Picture Library; 30 Mansell Collection; 31 Fotomas Index/The British Museum; 35 Giraudon; 34–35 Scala; 36 (top) Palazzo Vecchio/Scala; 36 (bottom) Fotomas Index; 37 Gabinetto Fotografico Sopr. Galleria, Florence; 38 (top) Anderson Roma; 38–39 Palazzo Ducale, Urbino; 39 (top) Orbis Publishing; 40–41 Alinari; 40 Orbis Publishing; 42 (top) Mary Evans Picture Library; 42 (bottom) Ronan Picture Library; 43 Mansell Collection; 44 Radio Times Hulton Picture Library; 46 (top) Radio Times Hulton Picture Library; 48 Radio Times Hulton Picture Library; 49 Courtesy of National Film Archive Stills Library; 50–51 RIBA; 52–53 Schweiz Landesbibliothek/Bibliotheque Nationale, Suisse; 52 (bottom) Radio Times Hulton Picture Library; 53 (bottom) Mansell Collection; 54 Ronan Picture Library; 56 Mansell Collection; 57 Louvre/Bulloz; 58 (top) Fotomas Index; 58 (bottom) Snark International/Bibliotheque Nationale; 59 Musée Carnavalet/Snark; 60 RIBA; 61–63 Bibliotheque Nationale, Paris; 64–65 RIBA; 66 Bulloz; 68 (top) Mansell Collection; 68 (bottom) Mary Evans Picture Library; 69 (top) British Museum; 69 (bottom) Bewick Collection/Newcastle upon Tyne Library; 70 (top) Musée Carnavalet/Bulloz; 70 (bottom) British Museum; 71 (bottom) Musée Carnavalet/Bulloz; 71 Ray Gardiner/British Museum; 72 Bewick Collection Newcastle upon Tyne Library; 73 Ray Gardiner/British Museum; 74–75 Mansell Collection; 77 Illustrated London News; 80 Mansell Collection; 82 Radio Times Hulton Picture Library; 83 Mary Evans Picture Library; 84 (bottom) Mansell Collection; 85 (top) Orbis Publishing; 85–6 (bottom) Radio Times Hulton Picture Library; 87 Ronan Picture Library; 88 Orbis Publishing; 89 (top) Brown Brothers Ltd; 89 (bottom) Fruitlands Museum Mass.; 90 (top) Snark International; 92 (bottom) Fotomas Index; 95 Illinois State Historical Society; 97 (top) Brown Brothers; 97 (bottom) Oneida Community Historical Committee; 98 (top) Shambaugh Collection, Iowa State Hist. Department; 99 (bottom) Bancroft Library; 100 Mansell Collection; 102 (top) Bulloz; 102 TUC Library; 103 Scala; 104 Bibliotheque Nationale, Suisse; 105 (bottom) Radio Times Hulton Picture Library; 107 Radio Times Hulton Picture Library; 108–109 Moscow State Gallery Tret'Jakor/Pucciarelli; 110–111 Radio Times Hulton Picture Library; Scala; 114 William Morris Gallery; 115 Radio Times Hulton Picture Library; 116–117 Manchester City Art Gallery; 118 Royal Town Planning Institute; 120 Royal Town Planning Institute; 121 (top) Radio Times Hulton Picture Library; 121–123 Royal Town Planning Institute; 124 Mansell Collection; 125 RIBA; 126 RIBA; 128 (top) Ville de Lyon Musée des Beaux Arts; 128–130 RIBA; 131 (left) E. Jesi Collection Milan/Fratelli Fabbri; 131 (right) Museo Civico, Como/Fratelli Fabbri; 132 Museo Civico, Como/Fratelli Fabbri; 133 RIBA; 134 Orbis Publishing; 135 (top) Orbis Publishing; 135 (bottom) RIBA; 137–139 Foundation le Corbusier; 140–143 Cosanti Foundation/Ivan Pintar; 143 (bottom) Archigram; 144–145 Archigram; 147 Buckminster Fuller; 148 Shensi Province China/Arts Council of Great Britain; 151 (top) Courtesy of National Film Archive Stills Library; 151 (bottom) by courtesy of Communitas by Paul and Percival Goodman; 152 Milton Keynes Corporation.

We are particularly grateful to the following: Mr G. Cornwall, the late Mr James Klugmann, and Messrs Vaisey & Turner for contributing the following illustrations: Mr G. Cornwall 79 (top, bottom and right); Mr J. Klugmann 46 (bottom), 47, 71 (top), 76, 84 (top), 90 (bottom), 91, 92 (top), 93, 105 (top); Messrs Vaisey & Turner 78.